Tolley's
Capital Gains Tax
2008
Post-Budget Supplement

by

Kevin Walton BA (Hons)

Members of the LexisNexis Group worldwide

United Kingdom	LexisNexis, a Division of Reed Elsevier (UK) Ltd, Halsbury House, 35 Chancery Lane, London, WC2A 1EL, and London House, 20-22 East London Street, Edinburgh EH7 4BQ
Argentina	LexisNexis Argentina, Buenos Aires
Australia	LexisNexis Butterworths, Chatswood, New South Wales
Austria	LexisNexis Verlag ARD Orac GmbH & Co KG, Vienna
Benelux	LexisNexis Benelux, Amsterdam
Canada	LexisNexis Butterworths, Markham, Ontario
Chile	LexisNexis Chile Ltda, Santiago
China	LexisNexis China, Beijing and Shanghai
France	LexisNexis SA, Paris
Germany	LexisNexis Deutschland GmbH, Munster
Hong Kong	LexisNexis Butterworths, Hong Kong
India	LexisNexis India, New Delhi
Italy	Giuffrè Editore, Milan
Japan	LexisNexis Japan, Tokyo
Malaysia	Malayan Law Journal Sdn Bhd, Kuala Lumpur
Mexico	LexisNexis Mexico, Mexico
New Zealand	LexisNexis Butterworths, Wellington
Poland	Wydawnictwo Prawnicze LexisNexis Sp, Warsaw
Singapore	LexisNexis Butterworths, Singapore
South Africa	LexisNexis Butterworths, Durban
USA	LexisNexis, Dayton, Ohio

© Reed Elsevier (UK) Ltd 2008

Published by LexisNexis

This is a Tolley title

A CIP Catalogue record for this book is available from the British Library.

ISBN 978 07545 3450 1

Printed and bound in Great Britain by Hobbs the Printers Ltd, Totton, Hampshire

Visit LexisNexis at www.lexisnexis.co.uk

About This Supplement

This Supplement to Tolley's Capital Gains Tax 2007/08 gives details of changes in the law and practice of capital gains tax and corporation tax on chargeable gains from 2 July 2007 to 11 March 2008. It lists the changes in the same order and under the same paragraph headings as the annual publication. Also included is a summary of the Chancellor's Budget proposals.

Each time Tolley's Capital Gains Tax 2007/08 is used, reference should be made to the material contained in this Supplement. The *Contents* give a list of all the chapters and paragraphs which have been updated.

Contents

This Supplement contains amendments to the chapters and paragraphs of Tolley's Capital Gains Tax 2007/08 as listed below.

Contents

Contents

1 Introduction

1.1A   The following new section is added after **1.1**.

'**Proposed capital gains tax reform.** A major reform of capital gains tax was announced in the 2007 Pre-Budget Report. The proposed changes are to apply to disposals on or after 6 April 2008 and will **not** apply for the purposes of corporation tax on chargeable gains. The changes are as follows.

- A single tax rate of 18% will apply to individuals, trustees and personal representatives.

- TAPER RELIEF (**61**) will be withdrawn both for disposals on or after 6 April 2008 and deferred gains coming into charge on or after that date.

- Indexation allowance (see **34** INDEXATION) will be withdrawn.

- All ASSETS HELD ON **31 MARCH 1982** (**8**) will be deemed to have been acquired on that date at market value on that date (i.e. rebasing will apply automatically to all assets).

- The relief for deferred charges on gains before 31 March 1982 (see **8.12** ASSETS HELD ON **31 MARCH 1982**) will be withdrawn.

- As a consequence of the above changes it will be possible to introduce simplified identification rules for shares and securities (see **59.1** SHARES AND SECURITIES—IDENTIFICATION RULES).

(2007 Pre-Budget Report Notice 17, 9 October 2007).

The Chancellor subsequently announced a further reform, also to apply to disposals on or after 6 April 2008. A new entrepreneurs' relief will apply to charge capital gains tax at an effective rate of 10% on up to the first £1 million of lifetime capital gains on disposals of trading businesses and of certain shares in trading companies (where the taxpayer owns at least 5% of the shares in the company and is able to exercise at least 5% of the voting rights). (HMRC Press Notice, 24 January 2008; HMRC Technical Note, 29 February 2008).

Draft legislation relating to the above changes has been published on the HMRC website.'

2 Annual Rates and Exemptions

2.1   The following paragraph is added at the end.

'**Proposed introduction of single CGT rate for 2008/09 onwards.** The Government has announced that it intends to introduce a single rate of capital gains tax of 18% for 2008/09 onwards. The rate will apply to disposals by individuals, personal representatives and trustees. (2007 Pre-Budget Report Notice 17, 9 October 2007).'

2.2   **Rates of tax — personal representatives etc.** The following sentence is added at the end.

'See **2.1** above for the proposed single rate of capital gains tax for 2008/09 onwards.'

3 Anti-Avoidance

3.2   **Disclosure of tax avoidance schemes.** The following paragraph is added after the second paragraph.

'HMRC have issued a technical note containing proposals to amend the disclosure provisions to rectify seven problem areas. (HMRC Technical Note 'Tax Avoidance Disclosure Regime — improving the scheme reference number system' 20 November 2007).'

The following is added immediately after list item (c) towards the foot of page 12.

'(ca) arrangements which are debtor repos, debtor quasi-repos, creditor repos or creditor quasi-repos within *FA 2007, Sch 13*;'

A reference to *SI 2007 No 2484, Art 4* is added to the statutory reference at the top of page 14.

The section headed 'Pre-disclosure enquiries' on page 17 is replaced by the following.

'*Pre-disclosure enquiries.* If HMRC suspects that a person is the promoter of a proposal or arrangements which may be notifiable under the above provisions, they may, by written notice, require that person to state whether in his opinion notification is required, and if not, the reasons for his opinion. In giving those reasons, it is not sufficient to indicate that a lawyer or other professional has given an opinion. The recipient of a notice must comply with it within the ten days beginning on the day after that on which the notice is issued.

If HMRC receive a statement (whether or not in response to a notice) giving reasons why a proposal or arrangements are not notifiable, they may apply to the Special Commissioners for an order requiring specified further information or documents to be provided in support of the reasons. The information or documents must be provided within the 14 days beginning on the day after that on which the order is made.

[*FA 2004, ss 313A, 313B; FA 2007, s 108(5); SI 2004 No 1864, Reg 8A; SI 2007 No 2153, Reg 4*].'

The following replaces the final paragraph starting on page 17 and the first complete paragraph on page 18.

'They can also apply to the Special Commissioners for an order that a proposal or arrangements be treated as notifiable. Again, the application must specify both the proposal or arrangements concerned and the promoter. Before making such an order, the Special Commissioners must be satisfied that HMRC have taken all reasonable steps (which need not include making use of the pre-disclosure enquiry provisions above) to establish whether the proposal or arrangements are notifiable and have reasonable grounds for suspecting that they may be notifiable. Grounds for suspicion may include an attempt by the promoter to avoid or delay providing information or documents under the pre-disclosure enquiry provisions and failure to comply with a requirement under those provisions in relation to other proposals or arrangements. The disclosure required as a result of an order under this provision must be made within the ten days beginning on the day after that on which the order is made. [*FA 2004, s 306A; FA 2007, s 108(2); SI 2004 No 1864, Reg 4(1A); SI 2007 No 2153, Reg 3(4)*].

Supplementary information. Where HMRC believe that a disclosure by a promoter has not included all the information required to be disclosed they can apply to the Special Commissioners for an order requiring the promoter to provide specified information or documents. Before making an order, the Special Commissioners must be satisfied that HMRC have reasonable grounds for suspecting that the information or documents form part of, or will support or explain, the required information. Information or documents required by an order under this provision must be provided within the ten days beginning on the day after that on which the order is made. [*FA 2004, s 308A; FA 2007, s 108(4); SI 2004 No 1864, Reg 4(3A); SI 2007 No 2153, Reg 3(5)*].'

3.18   **Restrictions on company reconstructions.** In the second paragraph, the case reference is updated to '*Snell v HMRC Ch D, [2007] STC 1279*'.

The following replaces the fourth paragraph.

'Applications for clearance should be directed to the Clearance and Counteraction Team, Anti-Avoidance Group Intelligence, First Floor, 22 Kingsway, London, WC2B 6NR for the attention of Mohini Sawhney (or, if market-sensitive information is included, Eric Gardner). Applications may be faxed to 020-7438 4409 or emailed to reconstructions@hmrc.gsi.gov.uk (in both cases after telephoning Eric Gardner (on 020-7438 6585) if market-sensitive information is included). A hard copy need not then be sent. From 1 November 2002, only a single application need be made as above for clearances under any one or more of: *ICTA 1988, s 215* (demergers), *ICTA 1988, s 225* (purchase of own shares), *ITA 2007, s 701* or *ICTA 1988, s 707* (transactions in securities), *TCGA 1992, s 138(1)* (as above), *TCGA 1992, s 139(5)* (reconstructions involving the transfer of a business — see **13.10** COMPANIES), *TCGA 1992, s 140B* (transfer or division of a UK business between EU member states — **45.10** OVERSEAS MATTERS), *TCGA 1992, s 140D* (transfer or division of a non-UK business between EU member states — **45.11** OVERSEAS MATTERS) and *FA 2002, Sch 29 para 88* (various clearances under the corporation tax intangible assets regime). (Before 1 November 2002, applications under *section 138(1)* were sent to Capital and Savings division at Solihull.) (Revenue Internet Statement 23 October 2002).'

3.22   **Dividend stripping.** The following replaces the second paragraph.

'Where a company (the 'first company') holds 10% or more of a class of shares in another company (the 'second company') otherwise than as a dealing company, and a distribution is or has been made to the first company which materially reduces or has reduced the value of the holding, the distribution is to be treated as a depreciatory transaction under *TCGA 1992, s 176* (see **3.21** above) in relation to any disposal of the shares. This applies whether the disposal is by the first company or any other company to which the holding has been transferred under the provisions of *TCGA 1992, s 140A* (transfer or division of UK business between companies in different EC member states, see **45.10** OVERSEAS M ATTERS), *s 171* (transfers within a group, see **27.2** GROUPS OF COMPANIES) or *s 172* (now repealed — see **45.3** OVERSEAS MATTERS). If the first and second companies are not members of the same group, they are deemed to be so.'

4   Appeals

4.11   **General Commissioners: preparation for hearing.** The following paragraph is added after the first paragraph.

'*General power to give directions.* with effect from 28 January 2008, the Commissioner(s) have wide direction-giving powers, on the application of any of the parties to proceedings or of their own motion. Applications by the parties (otherwise than during the hearing) must be in writing to the Clerk, and if not made with the consent of all the parties, must be served by the Clerk on any affected party, who may object. [*SI 1994 No 1812, Reg 3A; SI 2007 No 3612, Reg 5*].'

4.12   **General Commissioners: hearing and determination of proceedings.** The second paragraph is amended to read as follows.

'*Preliminary hearing.* With effect from 29 January 2008, a Commissioner may, on the application of a party or on his own initiative, hold a preliminary hearing to secure the just, expeditious and economical conduct of the proceedings, to ensure that the parties make all such admissions and agreements as ought reasonably to be made and to determine any preliminary question of fact or law which appears to be in issue. The Clerk must normally give the parties 14 days notice of such a hearing. Where the determination of the preliminary question substantially disposes of the proceedings, the Commissioners may treat the preliminary hearing as the substantive hearing. [*SI 1994 No 1812, Reg 3B; SI 2007 No 3612, Reg 5*]. Previously, preliminary points were considered prior to the hearing of the substantive appeal only in cases where the facts were complicated and the legal issue was short and easily decided (*Investment Trust v CIR (Sp C 173), [1998] SSCD 287*).'

4 Appeals

4.19   **Special Commissioners: hearing and determination of proceedings.** The following replaces the first paragraph on page 59,

'For cases in which costs/expenses were awarded against HMRC, see *Scott and another (trading as Farthings Steak House) v McDonald (Sp C 91)*, *[1996] SSCD 381*, *Robertson v CIR (No 2) (Sp C 313)*, *[2002] SSCD 242*, *Carvill v Frost (Sp C 447)*, *[2005] SSCD 208* and *Oriel Support Ltd v HMRC (Sp C 615)*, *[2007] SSCD 670.*'

4.28   The following new section is added at the end of the chapter.

'**New Appeal Tribunals.** Under the *Tribunals, Courts and Enforcement Act 2007*, the General and Special Commissioners are to be abolished. Tax appeals will instead be brought within a new unified system of tribunals created by the Act to take over a wide range of existing tribunal functions. Capital gains tax and corporation tax appeals will in most cases be heard by a First-tier Tribunal within a chamber specialising in tax matters. Appeals against the decisions of the First-tier Tribunal, with permission and on a point of law, will be to an Upper Tribunal. Appeals from the Upper Tribunal will be to the Court of Appeal or the Court of Session.

It is expected that tax appeals will be transferred to the new tribunals in April 2009.

HMRC has issued a consultation document seeking opinions on the administration of appeals to the tribunals and on whether to introduce a formal system under which an internal review of a decision would have to be carried out prior to any appeal hearing.

(HMRC Consultation Document 'Tax Appeals against decisions made by HMRC', October 2007).'

8   Assets held on 31 March 1982

8.1   **Re-basing to 31 March 1982.** The second paragraph is replaced by the following.

'The Government has announced that, for disposals on or after 6 April 2008, re-basing will apply for capital gains tax purposes automatically to all assets held on 31 March 1982. This change will not apply for the purposes of corporation tax on chargeable gains. (2007 Pre-Budget Report Notice 17, 9 October 2007).

A 50% reduction is made in taxing certain deferred gains (except, in certain cases, where the deferred gain is never deemed to accrue at all) which arise after 5 April 1988 where such gains are wholly or partly attributable to an increase in value of an asset before 31 March 1982; see **8.12** below. This relief is to be withdrawn, for capital gains tax purposes only, for disposals on or after 6 April 2008. The withdrawal will not apply for the purposes of corporation tax on chargeable gains. (2007 Pre-Budget Report Notice 17, 9 October 2007).'

8.7   **Previous no gain/no loss disposals.** List item (i) is replaced by the following.

'(i)   *TCGA 1992, s 58* (transfers between spouses living together, see **42.4 MARRIED PERSONS AND CIVIL PARTNERS**), *s 73* (reversion of settled property to settlor on death of person entitled to life interest, see **57.17 SETTLEMENTS**), *s 139* (company reconstructions, see **13.10 COMPANIES**), *s 140A* (transfer or division of UK business between companies in different EC member states, see **45.10 OVERSEAS MATTERS**), *s 140E* (European cross-border merger: assets left within UK tax charge, see **45.11A OVERSEAS MATTERS**), *s 171* (intra-group disposals of assets, see **27.2 GROUPS OF COMPANIES**), *s 172* (transfer of UK branch or agency before 1 April 2000, see **45.3 OVERSEAS MATTERS**), *s 211* (insurance business transfer schemes), *s 215* (amalgamation of building societies, see **13.10 COMPANIES**), *s 216* (transfer of building society's business to company, see **13.10 COMPANIES**), *s 217A* (transfer of assets on incorporation of registered friendly society, see **22.48** EXEMPTIONS AND RELIEFS), *ss 218–220* (housing associations, see **22.50** EX-EMPTIONS AND RELIEFS), *s 221* (harbour authorities, see **22.74** EXEMPTIONS AND RELIEFS), *s 257(2)* (gifts to charities etc., see **10.5** CHARITIES), *s 257(3)* (gifts to charities etc. out of settlements, see **10.6** CHARITIES), *s 258(4)* (gifts of national heritage property, see **22.81** EXEMPTIONS AND RELIEFS), *s 259(2)* (gifts to housing associations, see **22.50** EXEMPTIONS AND RELIEFS), *s 264* (transfers between constituency associations, see **22.68** EXEMPTIONS AND RELIEFS) and *s 267(2)* (sharing of transmission facilities, see **13.10** COMPANIES);'

8.12   **Deferred charges on gains before 31 March 1982.** The following is added to the first paragraph.

'This relief is to be withdrawn, for capital gains tax purposes only, for disposals on or after 6 April 2008. The withdrawal will not apply for the purposes of corporation tax on chargeable gains. (2007 Pre-Budget Report Notice 17, 9 October 2007).'

12   Claims

12.8   **Claim for restitution of payment made under mistake of law.** The case reference in the final paragraph is updated to read '*Monro v HMRC Ch D, [2007] STC 1182*'.

13   Companies

13.10   **Anti-avoidance, disapplication of relief and advance clearance.** The second paragraph is amended to read as follows.

'Applications for clearance should be directed to the Clearance and Counteraction Team, Anti-Avoidance Group Intelligence, First Floor, 22 Kingsway, London, WC2B 6NR for the attention of Mohini Sawhney (or, if market-sensitive information is included, Eric Gardner). Applications may be faxed to 020-7438 4409 or emailed to reconstructions@hmrc.gsi.gov.uk (in both cases after telephoning Eric Gardner (on 020-7438 6585) if market-sensitive information is included). A hard copy need not then be sent. From 1 November 2002, only a single application need be made as above for clearances under any one or more of: *ICTA 1988, s 215* (demergers), *ICTA 1988, s 225* (purchase of own shares), *ITA 2007, s 701* or *ICTA 1988, s 707* (transactions in securities), *TCGA 1992, s 138(1)* (share exchanges — see **3.18** ANTI-AVOIDANCE), *TCGA 1992, s 139(5)* (as above), *TCGA 1992, s 140B* (transfer or division of a UK business between EU member states — **45.10** OVERSEAS MATTERS), *TCGA 1992, s 140D* (transfer or division of a non-UK business between EU member states — **45.11** OVERSEAS MATTERS) and *FA 2002, Sch 29 para 88* (various clearances under the corporation tax intangible assets regime). (Before 1 November 2002, applications under *section 139(5)* were sent to Capital and Savings division at Solihull.) (Revenue Internet Statement 23 October 2002).'

13.11   **Overseas matters.** The final three paragraphs are amended to read as follows.

'Where a UK resident company transfers all or part of a trade carried on by it outside the UK to a company not resident in the UK in exchange, wholly or partly, for shares, see **45.9** OVERSEAS MATTERS. Where the transferee company is resident in an EC member state, see **45.11** OVERSEAS MATTERS. Where a UK company's business is carried on in the UK and is transferred to a company resident in another EC member state, see **45.10** OVERSEAS MATTERS. For European cross-border mergers, see **45.11A** OVERSEAS MATTERS.

There are 'exit charges' and provisions for the recovery of unpaid tax where a company ceases to be UK resident etc., is a dual resident company or is not resident in the UK. See **45.12** and **45.13** OVERSEAS MATTERS.

13   Companies

See also **13.18** below as regards European Companies (SEs) and **13.19** below as regards European Co-operatives (SCEs).'

13.16   **Demergers**. The following paragraph is added at the end.

'See also **45.10**, **45.11** OVERSEAS MATTERS for division of a business between companies in different EC member states.'

13.18   **European Company (Societas Europaea).** The text is amended to read as follows.

'*Council Regulation (EC) No 2157/2001* provided for the creation of a new type of company, the European Company or *Societas Europaea* ('SE'). The *Regulation* came into effect on 8 October 2004. It permits the formation of new SEs and also allows for the 'transformation' of existing companies into SEs and for the merger between two (or more) companies in different member states into an SE. For most tax purposes, an SE based in the UK is treated like a UK-resident plc, but special provisions are required to deal with, among other matters, the formation of SEs by cross-border merger. The provisions are intended to be broadly tax-neutral. (Revenue Technical Note, 'Implementation of the European Company Statute', January 2005).

Formation of SE by merger. See **45.11A** OVERSEAS MATTERS.

Residence. For the residence for tax purposes of an SE transferring its registered office to the UK, see **52.6** RESIDENCE AND DOMICILE.

Continuity on ceasing to be UK resident. If at any time a company ceases to be resident in the UK in the course of the formation of an SE by merger (whether or not the company continues to exist following the merger), *FA 1998, Sch 18* (company RETURNS (**54.18**), ASSESS-MENTS (**5**), APPEALS (**4**), etc.) applies after that time in relation to liabilities accruing and other matters arising before that time as if the company were still UK-resident and, if the company has ceased to exist, as if the SE were the company.

Where an SE transfers its registered office outside the UK and ceases to be UK-resident, *FA 1998, Sch 18* applies after that time in relation to liabilities accruing and other matters arising before that time as if the SE were still UK-resident.

[*F(No 2)A 2005, s 61*].

Groups of companies. See **27.1** GROUPS OF COMPANIES.'

13.19   The existing text is replaced by the following.

'**European Co-operative (Societas Co-operative Europaea).** *Council Regulation (EC) No 1435/2003* provided for the creation of a new type of co-operative, the European Co-operative or *Societas Co-operative Europaea* ('SCE'). The *Regulation* came into effect on 18 August 2006. It permits the formation of new SCEs and also allows for the 'transformation' of existing co-operatives into SEs and for the merger between two (or more) co-operatives in different member states into an SCE. For most tax purposes, an SCE based in the UK is treated like a registered industrial and provident society, but special provisions are required to deal with, among other matters, the formation of SCEs by cross-border merger.

Formation of SCE by merger. See **45.11A** OVERSEAS MATTERS.

Residence. For the residence for tax purposes of an SE transferring its registered office to the UK, see **52.6** RESIDENCE AND DOMICILE.'

14   Companies — Corporate Finance and Intangibles

14.3   **Loan relationships — summary of provisions.** A reference to *SI 2007 No 3431, Reg 2* is added at the end of the list of statutory references at the end of the paragraph headed, 'Foreign exchange gains and losses'.

14.5   **Definition of 'loan relationship'.** The following paragraph is inserted after the seventh paragraph on page 168.

'The 2008 Finance Bill is to include provisions to bring all life insurance policies and life annuity contracts to which a company is a party (other than protection-type policies) within the loan relationships provisions (2007 Pre-Budget Report Notice 10, 9 October 2007).'

14.13   **Intangible fixed assets.** The first complete paragraph on page 188 is amended to read as follows.

'Assets acquired by means of certain no gain/no loss transfers made after 27 June 2002 are excluded from the intangible assets regime in the hands of the transferee company if they fell outside the regime in the hands of the transferor company. The transfers in question are those within *TCGA 1992, s 139* (company reconstructions involving transfer of business — see **13.10** COMPANIES), *TCGA 1992, s 140A* (transfer of UK business between companies resident in different EC member states — see **45.10** OVERSEAS MATTERS) or *TCGA 1992, s 140E* (European cross-border merger: assets left within UK tax charge — see **45.11A** OVERSEAS MATTERS).'

A reference to *SI 2007 No 3186, Sch 1 para 24* is added to the list of statutory references at the end.

14.14   **Definition of 'intangible fixed asset'.** List items (*k*) and (*n*) are amended to read as follows.

'(*k*)   an asset held by a film production company to the extent that it represents production expenditure on a film to which *FA 2006, Sch 4* (taxation of activities of film production company in relation to films that commence principal photography on or after 1 January 2007) applies;

(*n*)   (except in relation to royalties) an asset representing expenditure on the production of, or on the acquisition before 31 March 2008 of, the original master version (as defined) of a film to which *FA 2006, Sch 4* does not apply;'

A reference to *SI 2007 No 1050, Reg 8* is added to the list of statutory references immediately before the penultimate paragraph.

15   Computation of Gains and Losses

15.1   **Basic principles.** The following is added to the fourth paragraph.

'See also *Crusader v HMRC (Sp C 640), 2007 STI 2418*, where an amount paid to a charity by the purchaser of a company was held to form part of the consideration for the sale of the company.'

The following paragraph is added at the end.

'**Proposed capital gains tax reforms.** See **1.1A** INTRODUCTION for capital gains tax changes proposed by the Government for disposals on or after 6 April 2008.'

15.2   **Disposal.** The following paragraph is added at the end.

'See also *Underwood v HMRC, Ch D [2008] EWHC 108 (Ch), 2008 STI 219.*'

15.4   **Allowable expenditure—general provisions.** The first paragraph of (*a*) is amended to read as follows.

'(*a*)   **The amount or value of the consideration, in money or money's worth, given wholly and exclusively for the acquisition of the asset** (plus 'incidental costs') or expenditure incurred wholly and exclusively in providing the asset [*TCGA 1992, s 38(1)(a)*].

In *Drummond v HMRC (Sp C 617), [2007] SSCD 682*, an individual (D) contracted to purchase five life assurance policies for a stated consideration of £1,962,233. On the following day he asked the vendor to surrender the policies. In his tax return, he claimed that the effect of this was that he had made an allowable loss of £1,962,233 for CGT purposes. HMRC rejected the claim on the basis that the £1,962,233 had not been incurred 'wholly and exclusively for the acquisition of any asset' but had been incurred 'to facilitate a tax avoidance scheme'. The Special Commissioner dismissed D's appeal, finding that the purported transactions were 'a charade', and that D had not acquired the rights to the policies as an investment but as part of a 'tax avoidance strategy'.

See also *Cleveleys Investment Trust Co v CIR (No 2) CS 1975, 51 TC 26; Allison v Murray Ch D 1975, 51 TC 57; Garner v Pounds Shipowners & Shipbreakers Ltd (and related appeal) HL 2000, 72 TC 561*.'

The text of (*b*) is amended to read as follows.

'(*b*)   **Expenditure wholly and exclusively incurred for the purpose of enhancing the value of the asset being expenditure reflected in the state or nature of the asset at the time of disposal.** [*TCGA 1992, s 38(1)(b)*]. Expenditure on initial repairs (including decoration) to a property, undertaken to put it into a fit state for letting, and not allowable in computing taxable property business profits, is regarded as allowable expenditure under this heading (HMRC Statement of Practice D24).

HMRC consider that capital contributions made to a company by shareholders are not normally allowable expenditure under this heading, but that if made at the time of issue of the shares they might be treated as in the nature of a share premium (ICAEW Guidance Note TR 713, 23 August 1988 and HMRC Capital Gains Manual CG 43500–43502). This view was upheld in *Trustees of the FD Fenston Will Trusts v HMRC, (Sp C 589), [2007] SSCD 316*. See also **15.6**(*a*) below.

'*Expenditure*' does not include the value of personal labour and skill (*Oram v Johnson Ch D 1980, 53 TC 319*). However, it may be in the form of providing money's worth and may be first reflected in the state or nature of the asset before completion even if this is after the time of disposal (*Chaney v Watkis Ch D 1985, 58 TC 707*).'

15.6   **Non-allowable expenditure.** The case reference in the last paragraph of (g) is updated to *HMRC v Smallwood CA, [2007] STC 1237*.

---

17   Corporate Venturing Scheme

17.6   **Number of employees requirement.** The following paragraph is added at the end of the section.

'HMRC consider that a full-time employee is one whose standard working week (excluding lunch breaks and overtime) is at least 35 hours (HMRC Venture Capital Schemes Manual VCM 15105).'

---

19   Double Tax Relief

19.2   **Double tax agreements.** The first paragraph of the Notes, headed 'Agreements not yet in force' is amended to read as follows.

'The above-mentioned Agreement with Belarus had not yet entered into force at 1 April 2002. (Revenue Tax Bulletin June 2002 p 940). A new agreement was signed with France on 28 January 2004. A new agreement was signed with Macedonia on 8 November 2006 (see *SI 2007 No 2127*) and applies in the UK from 1 April 2008 for corporation tax and from 6 April 2008 for capital gains tax. A new agreement was signed with the Faroe Islands on 20 June

2007 (see *SI 2007 No 3469*). A comprehensive agreement with Saudi Arabia was signed on 31 October 2007. A protocol to the agreement with New Zealand was signed on 7 November 2007. A comprehensive agreement with Moldova was signed on 8 November 2007. A comprehensive agreement with Slovenia was signed on 13 November 2007.'

The paragraph of the Notes headed 'Yugoslavia' is amended to read as follows.

'The Agreement published as *SI 1981 No 1815* between the UK and Yugoslavia is regarded as remaining in force between the UK and, respectively, Bosnia-Herzegovina, Croatia, Slovenia, Macedonia and Serbia and Montenegro. (HMRC Statements of Practice 3/04, 3/07). See above for the new agreements signed with Macedonia in 2006 and with Slovenia in 2007.'

20   Employee Share Schemes

20.2   **Extended meaning of 'shares'.** A reference to *SI 2007 No 2130* is added to the penultimate paragraph.

21   Enterprise Investment Scheme

21.3   **The use of money raised requirement.** The following paragraph is added before the final paragraph.

'In *GC Trading Ltd v HMRC (Sp C 630), 2007 STI 2231*, this condition was held to be satisfied even though the money raised was loaned to another company before being used to purchase a qualifying trade. On the evidence, the loans were the equivalent of a bank deposit and were simply the means used to preserve the money needed to acquire the trade.'

21.5   **The number of employees requirement.** The following paragraph is added at the end.

'HMRC consider that a full-time employee is one whose standard working week (excluding lunch breaks and overtime) is at least 35 hours (HMRC Venture Capital Schemes Manual VCM 15105).'

21.15   **Reinvestment into EIS shares after 5 April 1998.** The following paragraphs are added immediately before the heading 'Postponement of the original gain' on page 311.

'In *GC Trading Ltd v HMRC (Sp C 630), 2007 STI 2231*, the condition in (g) above was held to be satisfied even though the money raised was loaned to another company before being used to purchase a qualifying trade. On the evidence, the loans were the equivalent of a bank deposit and were simply the means used to preserve the money needed to acquire the trade.

See also *Blackburn and another v HMRC Ch D, [2008] EWHC 266 (Ch), 2008 STI 314*'.

21.17   **Reinvestment into EIS shares after 5 April 1998 — further provisions.** The following paragraph is added immediately before the heading 'Value received by the investor from the EIS company' on page 317.

'See also *Blackburn and another v HMRC Ch D, [2008] EWHC 266 (Ch), 2008 STI 314*.'

22   Exemptions and Reliefs

22.30   **Individual Savings Accounts (ISAs).** The text is amended to read as follows.

'ISAs are available **after 5 April 1999** to individuals over 18 (though see below) who are both resident and ordinarily resident in the UK and will continue to be available for a minimum of ten years. The accounts can be made up of cash, stocks and shares and, before 6 April 2005, life insurance (see below). They were introduced as a replacement for PEPs and TESSAs, although see **22.32** below as regards PEPs already in existence at the end of 1998/99 and note that neither the value of PEP holdings nor any capital transferred to an ISA from a TESSA (tax-exempt special savings account) will affect the amount which can be subscribed to an ISA. For 2008/09 onwards, investors can subscribe up to £7,200 to ISAs in each tax year, of which a maximum of £3,600 can be saved in cash with one provider. Previously, the overall investment maximum was £7,000 each tax year, of which a maximum of £3,000 could go into cash and, for 2004/05 and earlier years, £1,000 into life insurance. See further details below. After 5 April 2001, the availability of cash ISAs is extended to 16 and 17-year olds. There is no statutory lock-in, minimum subscription, minimum holding period or lifetime subscription limit. Withdrawals may be made at any time without loss of tax relief but not so as to allow further subscriptions in breach of the annual maximum.

Interest and dividends are free of income tax (and a 10% tax credit is payable on dividends received from UK equities before 6 April 2004). Gains arising from assets held within an ISA are not chargeable gains for CGT purposes (and losses are not allowable).

All remaining PEPs automatically become stocks and shares ISAs on 6 April 2008.

[*TCGA 1992, s 151; ICTA 1988, ss 333, 333A; FA 1998, ss 75, 76, Sch 27 Pt III(15); ITTOIA 2005, ss 694–701, Sch 1 paras 141, 436, 503*].

The Individual Savings Account Regulations 1998 (*SI 1998 No 1870* as amended) provide for the setting up by HMRC-approved accounts managers of plans in the form of an account (an ISA) under which individuals may make certain investments, for the conditions under which they may invest and under which the accounts are to operate, for relief from tax in respect of account investments, and for general administration. The regulations generally took effect on 6 April 1999 and are summarised below.

Eligibility. An application to subscribe to an ISA may be made by an individual who is 18 or over (though see below as regards children under 18) and who is resident and ordinarily resident in the UK (or who is a non-UK resident Crown employee performing duties treated under *ICTA 1988, s 132(4)(a)* (see Tolley's Income Tax) as performed in the UK or, after 5 April 2001. who is married to, or a civil partner of, such an employee). Joint accounts are not permitted. An investor who subsequently fails to meet the residence requirement may retain the account and the right to tax exemptions thereunder but can make no further subscriptions to the account until he again comes to meet that requirement. After 7 January 2003, an application made on behalf of an individual suffering from a mental disorder, by a parent, guardian, spouse, civil partner, son or daughter of his, is treated as if made by that individual. This replaced a rule specific to Scotland whereby a *curator bonis* appointed in respect of a qualifying individual incapable of managing his affairs could subscribe to an ISA in his capacity as such without affecting his right to subscribe in any other capacity.

Rules for accounts. For 2008/09 onwards, an individual can subscribe to a single cash account and/or a single stocks and shares account in each tax year. Up to £3,600 can be saved in the cash account. The remainder of the £7,200 allowance can be invested in the stocks and shares account with the same or another accounts manager. A cash account consists of a single cash component and a stocks and shares account consists of a single stocks and shares component. For details of investments qualifying for inclusion in each component, see Tolley's Income Tax.

For 2007/08 and earlier years, an ISA is made up of *one or more* of the following: a stocks and shares component, a cash component and, for 2004/05 and earlier years, an insurance component. It must be designated from the outset as a maxi-account, mini-account or TESSA only account, such designation continuing to have effect for any year in which the investor makes a subscription to the account (but see above). The insurance component is abolished after 5 April 2005. After that date, life insurance products instead go into the stocks and shares component, except that certain low-risk products providing a 'cash-like' return go into the cash component. As regards insurance components in existence immediately before 6 April 2005, these are merged into either the stocks and shares component or the cash component, as appropriate. Where the insurance component was part of a maxi-account it is treated as merging on that date into the stocks and shares, or, as appropriate, cash component of that account. If the insurance component constituted a mini-account, it is treated as becoming on that date the stocks and shares, or, as appropriate, cash component of the same account.

A *maxi-account* must comprise a stocks and shares component (*with or without* other components). The maximum subscription per tax year (up to and including 2009/10) is £7,000 of which a maximum of £3,000 may be allocated to a cash component and, for 2004/05 and earlier years, £1,000 to an insurance component. In any tax year in which an investor subscribes to a maxi-account he cannot subscribe to any other ISA apart from a TESSA only account.

A *mini-account* must consist of a single specified component. The maximum subscription (per tax year) is £4,000 (£3,000 for 2004/05 and earlier years) if that component is stocks and shares, £3,000 if it is cash and, for 2004/05 and earlier years, £1,000 if it is insurance. In any tax year in which an investor subscribes to a mini-account, he cannot subscribe to another mini-account consisting of the same component or to a maxi-account.

A *TESSA only account* is an account consisting of a cash component only and limited to capital (*not* accumulated interest) transferred from a TESSA (see Tolley's Income Tax) within six months following its maturity after 5 April 1999 (or after 5 January 1999 where no follow-up TESSA is opened). Such transfers are not subject to any annual subscription limit, and may also be made to a maxi-account or to a cash component mini-account without counting towards the annual subscription limits for such accounts. Continuing subscriptions after 5 April 1999 to a TESSA or follow-up TESSA do not affect an individual's ISA annual subscription limits.

ISAs in existence immediately before 6 April 2008 are redesignated with effect from that date. TESSA only accounts and cash mini-accounts are treated as cash accounts from that date. Maxi-accounts consisting only of a stocks and shares component are treated as stocks and shares accounts. Maxi-accounts consisting of both a cash and a stocks and shares component are separated into a cash account and a stocks and shares account.

A PEP in existence immediately before 6 April 2008 is treated on and after that date as a stocks and shares account.

Subscriptions. Subscriptions to an ISA must be made in cash (and must be allocated irrevocably to the agreed component or single component) except that:

- shares acquired by the investor under a savings-related (SAYE) share option scheme (see **20.26** EMPLOYEE SHARE SCHEMES); or

- shares appropriated to him under an approved profit sharing scheme (see **20.29** EMPLOYEE SHARE SCHEMES); or

- plan shares (but not securities or other rights) of an approved share incentive plan (see **20.19** EMPLOYEE SHARE SCHEMES) which have ceased to be subject to the plan but remain in his beneficial ownership

may be transferred to a stocks and shares component. Such transfers count towards the annual subscription limits, by reference to the market value of the shares at the date of transfer. No chargeable gain or allowable loss arises on the transfer. A transfer of SAYE scheme shares must be made within 90 days after the exercise of the option. A transfer of shares appropriated under a profit sharing scheme must be made within 90 days after the earlier of the release date and the date on which the investor instructed the scheme trustees to transfer ownership of the shares to him. A transfer of share incentive plan shares must be made within 90 days after the shares ceased to be subject to the plan. In all cases, after 12 December 2000, 'shares' includes a reference to shares held in the form of depositary interests (see (*j*) below).

Investments. ISA investments cannot be purchased otherwise than out of cash held by the account manager and allocated to the particular component concerned, and cannot be purchased from the investor or his spouse or civil partner.

The title to ISA investments (other than cash deposits, national savings products and certain insurance policies) is vested in the account manager (or his nominee) either alone or jointly with the investor, though all ISA investments are in the beneficial ownership of the investor. The investor may elect to receive annual reports and accounts etc. in respect of ISA investments and/or to attend and vote at shareholders' etc. meetings.

Applications to subscribe to an ISA. The statements and declarations to be made when applying to subscribe to an ISA are specified. The maximum penalty for an incorrect statement or declaration is the amount (if any) of income tax and/or capital gains tax underpaid as a result. Assessments to withdraw tax relief or otherwise recover tax underpaid may be made on the account manager or investor. HMRC have power to require information from, and to inspect records of, account managers and investors.

Withdrawal of funds and transfer of accounts. From 1 October 2002 (and with reference to pre-existing ISAs as well as new ones), the terms and conditions of an ISA cannot prevent the investor from withdrawing funds or from transferring his account (or a part of it) to another HMRC-approved account manager (subject to the conditions governing such transfers). The account manager is allowed a reasonable business period (not exceeding 30 days) to comply with the investor's instructions in this regard. By concession, an ISA opened before 24 August 2002 offering a fixed or guaranteed return under terms requiring the funds to be locked in for a period of up to five years may, if the manager wishes and with HMRC agreement, continue to maturity under its original terms, though no further subscriptions can be made after 5 April 2003 (Revenue Press Release 26 July 2002). For 2008/09 onwards, it is possible to transfer both current year subscriptions and previous year subscriptions to a cash account into a stocks and shares account. Current year subscriptions so transferred do not then count towards the cash subscription limit for the year.

Children under 18. For 2001/02 onwards, 16 and 17-year olds who otherwise satisfy the general conditions above may subscribe to a cash account (for 2007/08 and earlier years a cash mini-account or cash component of a maxi-account). The maximum subscription for a tax year at the end of which the individual is under 18 is £3,600 (£3,000 for 2007/08 and earlier years). The maximum ISA subscriptions for the tax year in which the individual reaches 18 are the same as for any other 18-year old, but no more than £3,600 (£3,000 for 2007/08 and earlier years) can be subscribed before the individual's 18th birthday. See also under Tax Exemptions below.

Tax exemptions. Except as stated below, no income tax or capital gains tax is chargeable on the account manager or the investor in respect of interest, dividends, distributions, gains, (from 27 December 2005) alternative financial arrangement return or (from 1 January 2007) building society bonus on ISA investments. Capital losses are not allowable. As stated in the introduction above, tax credits on UK dividends paid before 6 April 2004 are repayable (via the account manager). An investor who ceases to be UK-resident is treated as continuing to be so resident as regards his entitlement to repayment of tax credits.

Interest on a cash deposit held within a stocks and shares component or insurance component is, however, taxable at the lower rate of income tax, such tax to be accounted for by the account manager (by set-off against tax repayments or otherwise). There is no further liability; the interest does not form part of the investor's total income and the tax paid cannot be repaid to the investor.

As regards children under 18 (see above), the exemption for interest on a cash account does not prevent the application of the settlements legislation of *ITTOIA 2005, s 629* (see Tolley's

Income Tax under Settlements) whereby (subject to a *de minimis* limit) the income of an unmarried minor on capital provided by a parent is taxable as if it were the parent's income. Such income arising in an ISA is therefore taxable.

Life assurance gains on policies held within an insurance component are not subject to income tax (and a deficiency on termination is not deductible from the investor's total income). If it comes to the account manager's notice that such a policy is invalid, i.e. its terms and conditions do not provide (or no longer provide) that it be held only as a qualifying insurance component investment, a chargeable event then occurs, with any gain taxable as income. If the policy has already terminated, the chargeable event is deemed to have occurred at the end of the final policy year (see Tolley's Income Tax). Any previous chargeable event which actually occurred in relation to the policy is similarly taxed, by reference to the time it occurred. Savings rate income tax (for 2004/05 and earlier years, basic rate income tax) is payable by the account manager (with HMRC also having power to assess the investor). Any higher rate tax due is payable by the investor by assessment within five years after 31 January following the year of assessment in which the chargeable event occurred or was deemed to occur. Top-slicing relief (see Tolley's Income Tax) is available in the same way as for non-ISA-related chargeable events.

Exempt income and gains do not have to be reported in the investor's personal tax return.

Further capital gains matters. A transfer of ISA investments by an account manager to an investor is deemed to be made at market value, with no capital gain or allowable loss arising. An investor is treated as holding shares or securities in an ISA in a capacity other than that in which he holds any other shares etc. of the same class in the same company, so that share identification rules (see **59.1** SHARES AND SECURITIES—IDENTIFICATION RULES) are applied separately to ISA investments (and separately as between different ISAs held by the same investor). The normal share reorganisation rules are disapplied in respect of ISA investments in the event of a reorganisation of share capital involving an allotment for payment, e.g. a rights issue. Shares transferred to an ISA in the limited circumstances described above are deemed for these purposes to have been ISA investments from,

● in the case of SAYE option scheme shares, their acquisition by the investor; or

● in the case of profit sharing scheme shares, the earlier of the release date and the date on which the investor instructed the scheme trustees to transfer ownership of the shares to him; or

● in the case of share incentive plan shares, the date when they ceased to be subject to the plan.

Where the investor held shares eligible for transfer to an ISA and other shares of the same class but not so eligible, disposals are generally identified primarily with the latter, thus preserving to the greatest possible extent the eligibility of the remaining shares.

Repairing of invalid accounts. There are provisions for the 'repairing' of certain incompatible accounts and excess subscriptions to prevent loss of ISA status and tax exemptions.

Account managers. The regulations cover qualification as an account manager, HMRC approval and withdrawal thereof, appointment of UK tax representatives of non-UK account managers, account managers ceasing to act or to qualify, claims for tax relief and agreement of liabilities, annual returns of income and of information, annual and interim tax repayment claims, record-keeping, and information to be provided to investors.

[*SI 1998 Nos 1870, 3174; SI 2000 Nos 809, 2079, 3112; SI 2001 No 908; SI 2001 No 3629, Arts 168–178; SI 2001 No 3778; SI 2002 Nos 453, 1974, 3158; SI 2003 No 2747; SI 2004 Nos 1677, 2996; SI 2005 Nos 609, 2561, 3230, 3350; SI 2006 No 3194; SI 2007 No 2119*].

Separate regulations modify existing tax legislation so far as it concerns individual savings account business of insurance companies. [*SI 1998 No 1871 as amended*].

Closure and death. Subject to the ISA terms and conditions, an investor may close an ISA at any time without affecting tax exemptions up to the date of closure. Where an investor dies, income and gains in respect of ISA investments which arise after the date of death but before the date of closure are not exempt.'

22.32   **Personal Equity Plans (PEPs).** The first paragraph is amended to read as follows.

'**Before 6 April 1999**, an individual could make, subject to conditions, investments under a plan and obtain exemption from capital gains tax (as well as income tax) in respect of transactions covered by the plan. No further subscriptions to PEPs can be made after 5 April 1999, but existing PEPs may continue, and independently of individual savings accounts (see **22.30** above) until 5 April 2008. With effect from 6 April 2008, continuing PEPs are brought within the ISA rules.'

22.48   **Friendly societies.** A reference to *SI 2007 No 2134* is added to the list of statutory references at the end.

22.58   **Scientific research associations.** The text is amended to read as follows.

'**Scientific research associations**, provided that in each case

(*a*)   its object is the undertaking of 'research and development' (within the meaning of *ICTA 1988, s 837A*) which may lead to or facilitate an extension of any class or classes of trade, and

(*b*)   it is prohibited by its Memorandum or similar instrument from distributing its income or property to its members in any form other than that of reasonable payments for supplies, labour, power, services, interest and rent.

For accounting periods beginning on or after 1 January 2008, Treasury regulations (see *SI 2007 No 3426*) prescribe circumstances in which associations are deemed to comply, or not to comply, with the above conditions.

For accounting periods beginning before 1 January 2008, the requirement at (*a*) above was that the association had as its object scientific research (i.e. research in the fields of natural or applied science) which could lead to an extension of trade and which was approved by the Department of Trade and Industry.

[*TCGA 1992, s 271(6)(b); ICTA 1988, s 508; F(No 2)A 2005, s 13; ITA 2007, Sch 1 para 100; SI 2007 Nos 3424, 3426*].'

22.66   **Companies.** The text of (*c*) is amended to read as follows.

'*Transfers or divisions of UK businesses between companies resident in different EC member states* are treated as if made at a no gain, no loss consideration. See **45.10** OVERSEAS MATTERS.'

23   Fraudulent or Negligent Conduct

23.8   **Investigatory powers.** The section headed 'HMRC use of Police and Criminal Evidence Act 1984 powers' is amended to read as follows.

'**HMRC use of Police and Criminal Evidence Act 1984 powers.** With effect from 1 December 2007, HMRC are able to exercise certain powers under the *Police and Criminal Evidence Act 1984* when conducting direct tax criminal investigations. Previously, such powers were available to HMRC only in relation to matters that were handled by HM Customs and Excise before the merger with the Inland Revenue in 2005. The powers involved include those concerning search warrants and arrest. Only HMRC officers authorised by the Commissioners for HMRC are able to exercise the powers. Similar powers are available to HMRC in Scotland and Northern Ireland.

As a result of the availability of the above police powers, the search and seizure powers at **23.10** below are no longer needed and are repealed with effect from 1 December 2007. The power to seek judicial authority to require the delivery of documents at **23.9** below is restricted to circumstances where the equivalent police power cannot be used because the material concerned is outside its scope.

[*Police and Criminal Evidence Act 1984, s 114; FA 2007, ss 82–87, Schs 22, 23; SI 2007 Nos 3166, 3175*].

See HMRC Technical Note 'Criminal investigation powers and safeguards', 30 November 2007.'

23.9   **Order for delivery of documents in serious tax fraud cases.** The second paragraph is amended to read as follows.

'With effect from 8 November 2007, these provisions are restricted to circumstances where the equivalent power under the *Police and Criminal Evidence Act 1984* (see **23.8** above) cannot be used because the material concerned cannot be obtained using those powers.'

The following paragraph is added at the end.

'[*TMA 1970, s 20BA, Sch 1AA; Police and Criminal Evidence Act 1984, s 14B; FA 2000, s 149, Sch 39; FA 2007, ss 82(6), 84(5); SI 2007 No 3166*].'

23.10   **Search and seizure.** The first three paragraphs are amended to read as follows.

'Before 1 December 2007, where there is a reasonable suspicion of serious tax fraud, and there are reasonable grounds for believing that use of the procedure under *TMA 1970, s 20BA* (see **23.9** above) might seriously prejudice the investigation, HMRC may apply to a Circuit judge (a sheriff in Scotland or a County Court judge in NI) for a warrant to enter premises within 14 days to search and seize any things which may be relevant as evidence. There are detailed procedural rules governing searches and the removal of documents etc.

These provisions are repealed (and replaced by equivalent powers under the *Police and Criminal Evidence Act 1984* — see **23.8** above) with effect from 1 December 2007.

[*TMA 1970, ss 20C, 20CC, 20D; FA 2007, s 84(4)–(6), Sch 22 para 4; SI 2007 No 3166*].'

27   Groups of Companies

27.1   **Definitions.** The following is added to the end of the first paragraph under the heading 'General' on page 376.

'For HMRC's interpretation of 'ordinary share capital', see HMRC Brief 54/2007.'

27.9   **Company leaving group after acquiring asset intra-group — degrouping charge.** The case reference in the third complete paragraph on page 384 is updated to *Johnston Publishing (North) Ltd v HMRC Ch D, [2007] STC 1481*.

The following replaces the first complete paragraph on page 385.

'Where, as part of a process of merger to which *TCGA 1992, s 140E* (European cross-border merger: assets left within UK tax charge — see **45.11A** OVERSEAS MATTERS) applies, a company which is a member of a group ceases to exist and as a consequence assets, or shares in one or more companies which were also members of the group, are transferred to the transferee, the company which has ceased to exist and any company whose shares have been transferred to the transferee are, for the purposes of these provisions, not treated as having left the group. The transferee and the company which ceased to exist are treated as the same entity and, if the transferee is itself a member of a group following the merger, any company which was a member of the first group and became a member of the transferee's group as a result of the merger is treated as if the two groups were the same. [*TCGA 1992, s 179(1B)–(1D); F(No 2)A 2005, s 64(4); SI 2007 No 3186, Sch 2 para 7*].

Where shares in a company are transferred on or after 1 January 2007 as part of the process of the transfer of a business to which *TCGA 1992, s 140A* (see **45.10** OVERSEAS MATTERS) or *TCGA 1992, s 140C* (see **45.11** OVERSEAS MATTERS) applies, and as a result, the company ceases to be a member of a group, it is treated as not having left the group. If the company becomes a member of a second group, of which the transferee company is a member, as a result of the transfer, the company is treated as if the two groups were the same. [*TCGA 1992, s 179(1AA); SI 2007 No 3186, Sch 1 para 9*].'

27.19   **Pre-change assets.** The first bulleted list on page 396 is amended to read as follows.

'●   *TCGA 1992, s 139* (reconstruction involving transfer of business — see **13.10** COMPANIES);

●   *TCGA 1992, s 140* (transfer of assets to non-resident company — see **45.9** OVERSEAS MATTERS);

●   *TCGA 1992, s 140A* (transfer or division of UK business between companies in different EC member states — see **45.10** OVERSEAS MATTERS);

●   *TCGA 1992, s 140E* (European cross-border merger leaving assets within UK tax charge — see **13.18** COMPANIES);

●   *TCGA 1992, ss 152, 153* (ROLLOVER RELIEF—REPLACEMENT OF BUSINESS ASSETS (**55**)); and

●   *TCGA 1992, s 187* (postponement of charge on deemed disposal on company ceasing to be UK resident — see **45.12** OVERSEAS MATTERS).'

27.21   **Definitions.** The penultimate paragraph is amended to read as follows.

'For discussion of *Sch 7A para 1(6)(7)* see *Five Oaks Properties Ltd v HMRC (and related appeals) (Sp C 563), [2006] SSCD 769* and *Limitgood Ltd v HMRC; HMRC v Prizedome Ltd; HMRC v Limitgood Ltd, Ch D [2008] EWHC 19 (Ch)*.'

28   HMRC: Administration

28.10   **Revenue functions carried out by the Assets Recovery Agency.** The final paragraph is amended to read as follows.

'The Assets Recovery Agency is to be merged with the Serious and Organised Crime Agency (see *Serious Crime Act 2007, s 74, Sch 8*).'

29   HMRC: Confidentiality of Information

29.2   **Tax authorities of other countries.** The third paragraph of (*c*) is amended to read as follows.

'With effect from 19 July 2006, the UK may enter into agreements with other countries for mutual assistance in the enforcement of taxes. Such agreements may include provision for the exchange of information forseeably relevant to the administration, enforcement or recovery of any UK tax or foreign tax. HMRC may disclose information under such agreements only if satisfied that the confidentiality rules applied by the foreign authorities concerned with respect to the information are no less strict than the equivalent UK rules. [*FA 2006, s 173*]. This power has been exercised to enter into the joint Council of Europe/Organisation for Economic Co-operation and Development Convention on Mutual Administrative Assistance in Tax Matters, signed on behalf of the UK on 24 May 2007. [*SI 2007 No 2126*].

The above power replaces similar powers to enter into tax information exchange agreements with other countries, which applied with effect from 28 July 2000 and were limited to income tax, capital gains tax and corporation tax, and foreign equivalents. Agreements made under those powers in force on 18 July 2006 are after that date treated as if made under the *FA 2006* powers. [*ICTA 1988, ss 815C, 816(2)(2ZA); FA 2000, s 146(1)(2); FA 2002, s 88(2)(3); FA 2003, s 198; FA 2006, s 173(8)–(10), Sch 26 Pt 8(2)*]. The *FA 2006* powers also replace provisions for double taxation agreements to include arrangements for the exchange of information relating to the taxes covered by the agreement. Again, such arrangements in force under an agreement on 18 July 2006 are treated after that date as if made under the *FA 2006* powers. [*ICTA1988, ss 788(2), 816(2); FA 2002, s 88(2)(3); FA 2003, s 198; FA 2006, s 173(8)–(10), Sch 26 Pt 8(2)*].

The UK signed a comprehensive tax information exchange agreement with Bermuda on 4 December 2007 (HMRC Press Notice 4 December 2007). For agreements in connection with the EU Savings Directive and special withholding tax, see **19.9 DOUBLE TAX RELIEF.'**

A new item is added at the end of the list as follows.

'(*p*)   **Criminal Assets Bureau in Ireland.** From 15 February 2008, HMRC may disclose information to the Criminal Assets Bureau in Ireland for the purpose of enabling or assisting the CAB to exercise any of its functions in connection with the proceeds of crime. [*Serious Crime Act 2007, s 85*].'

---

33   Hold-Over Reliefs

33.7   **Gifts on which inheritance tax is chargeable etc. after 13 March 1989.** The penultimate paragraph is amended to read as follows.

'Partial claims are not permitted. Where, however, a single transaction involves the transfer of a number of separate assets (i.e. where a separate chargeable gain accrues on each asset), a claim is required for each asset and the parties are free to choose which assets are to be the subject of a claim. (HMRC Capital Gains Manual CG 67180). In such circumstances, some gains can be left in charge to be covered by annual exemptions or losses etc.'

---

34   Indexation

34.1   **Indexation allowance.** The first paragraph is amended to read as follows.

'For the purposes of both capital gains tax and corporation tax on chargeable gains, an indexation allowance is deductible in certain circumstances from the unindexed gain. The Government has announced that indexation allowance is to be withdrawn, for capital gains tax purposes only, for disposals on or after 6 April 2008. This will not apply for the purposes of corporation tax on chargeable gains. (2007 Pre-Budget Report Notice 17, 9 October 2007).'

The updated RPI (Retail Prices Index) Table is as set out below.

	1982	1983	1984	1985	1986	1987	1988	1989	1990	1991
January	—	82.61	86.84	91.20	96.25	100.0	103.3	111.0	119.5	130.2
February	—	82.97	87.20	91.94	96.60	100.4	103.7	111.8	120.2	130.9
March	79.44	83.12	87.48	92.80	96.73	100.6	104.1	112.3	121.4	131.4
April	81.04	84.28	88.64	94.78	97.67	101.8	105.8	114.3	125.1	133.1
May	81.62	84.64	88.97	95.21	97.85	101.9	106.2	115.0	126.2	133.5
June	81.85	84.84	89.20	95.41	97.79	101.9	106.6	115.4	126.7	134.1
July	81.88	85.30	89.10	95.23	97.52	101.8	106.7	115.5	126.8	133.8
August	81.90	85.68	89.94	95.49	97.82	102.1	107.9	115.8	128.1	134.1
September	81.85	86.06	90.11	95.44	98.30	102.4	108.4	116.6	129.3	134.6
October	82.26	86.36	90.67	95.59	98.45	102.9	109.5	117.5	130.3	135.1
November	82.66	86.67	90.95	95.92	99.29	103.4	110.0	118.5	130.0	135.6

	1992	1993	1994	1995	1996	1997	1998	1999	2000	2001
January	135.6	137.9	141.3	146.0	150.2	154.4	159.5	163.4	166.6	171.1
February	136.3	138.8	142.1	146.9	150.9	155.0	160.3	163.7	167.5	172.0
March	136.7	139.3	142.5	147.5	151.5	155.4	160.8	164.1	168.4	172.2
April	138.8	140.6	144.2	149.0	152.6	156.3	162.6	165.2	170.1	173.1
May	139.3	141.1	144.7	149.6	152.9	156.9	163.5	165.6	170.7	174.2
June	139.3	141.0	144.7	149.8	153.0	157.5	163.4	165.6	171.1	174.4
July	138.8	140.7	144.0	149.1	152.4	157.5	163.0	165.1	170.5	173.3
August	138.9	141.3	144.7	149.9	153.1	158.5	163.7	165.5	170.5	174.0
September	139.4	141.9	145.0	150.6	153.8	159.3	164.4	166.2	171.7	174.6
October	139.9	141.8	145.2	149.8	153.8	159.5	164.5	166.5	171.6	174.3
November	139.7	141.6	145.3	149.8	153.9	159.6	164.4	166.7	172.1	173.6

	2002	2003	2004	2005	2006	2007	2008
January	173.3	178.4	183.1	188.9	193.4	201.6	209.8
February	173.8	179.3	183.8	189.6	194.2	203.1	
March	174.5	179.9	184.6	190.5	195.0	204.4	
April	175.7	181.2	185.7	191.6	196.5	205.4	
May	176.2	181.5	186.5	192.0	197.7	206.2	
June	176.2	181.3	186.8	192.2	198.5	207.3	
July	175.9	181.3	186.8	192.2	198.5	206.1	
August	176.4	181.6	187.4	192.6	199.2	207.3	
September	177.7	182.5	188.1	193.1	200.1	208.0	
October	177.9	182.6	188.6	193.3	200.4	208.9	
November	178.2	182.7	189.0	193.6	201.1	209.7	
December	178.5	183.5	189.9	194.1	202.7	210.9	

36   Interest on Overpaid Tax

36.1 **Persons other than companies.** Recent interest rates are as follows.

3.00% p.a. from 6 January 2008
4.00% p.a. from 6 August 2007 to 5 January 2008
3.00% p.a. from 6 September 2006 to 5 August 2007
2.25% p.a. from 6 September 2005 to 5 September 2006

36.2 **Companies.** Recent interest rates for accounting periods ending **on or after 1 July 1999** for amounts overpaid **on or after the normal due date** are as follows.

4.00% p.a. from 6 January 2008
5.00% p.a. from 6 August 2007 to 5 January 2008
4.00% p.a. from 6 September 2006 to 5 August 2007
3.00% p.a. from 6 September 2005 to 5 September 2006

Recent interest rates for accounting periods ending **on or after 1 July 1999** for amounts overpaid **before the normal due date**, for example under the quarterly accounting rules for large companies, are as follows.

5.00% p.a. from 18 February 2008
5.25% p.a. from 17 December 2007 to 17 February 2008
5.50% p.a. from 16 July 2007 to 16 December 2007
5.25% p.a. from 21 May 2007 to 15 July 2007
5.00% p.a. from 22 January 2007 to 20 May 2007
4.75% p.a. from 20 November 2006 to 21 January 2007
4.50% p.a. from 14 August 2006 to 19 November 2006
4.25% p.a. from 15 August 2005 to 13 August 2006

These rates apply up to the earlier of the date of repayment and the normal due date (after which the normal rates apply).

Recent interest rates for accounting periods ending **before 1 July 1999** are as follows.

2.75% p.a. from 6 January 2008
3.50% p.a. from 6 August 2007 to 5 January 2008
2.75% p.a. from 6 September 2006 to 5 August 2007
2.00% p.a. from 6 September 2005 to 5 September 2006

37   Interest and Surcharges on Unpaid Tax

37.1   **Persons other than companies —1996/97 onwards (self-assessment) and assessments raised after 5 April 1998.** Recent interest rates are as follows.

7.50% p.a. from 6 January 2008
8.50% p.a. from 6 August 2007 to 5 January 2008
7.50% p.a. from 6 September 2006 to 5 August 2007
6.50% p.a. from 6 September 2005 to 5 September 2006

37.4   **Surcharges on unpaid tax.** The following paragraph is added at the end.

'Legislation is to be introduced in the 2008 Finance Bill to allow HMRC to waive surcharges (and interest) on tax paid late due to the severe flooding in the Summer of 2007. In the period before the legislation is enacted, HMRC will exercise their discretionary power not to collect interest and surcharges in such circumstances.' (HMRC News Release, 25 July 2007).

37.5   **Companies.** Recent interest rates for accounting periods ending **on or after 1 July 1999** for tax becoming due **on or after the normal due date** are as follows.

7.50% p.a. from 6 January 2008
8.50% p.a. from 6 August 2007 to 5 January 2008
7.50% p.a. from 6 September 2006 to 5 August 2007
6.50% p.a. from 6 September 2005 to 5 September 2006

Recent interest rates for accounting periods ending **on or after 1 July 1999** for tax payable **before the normal due date** under the quarterly accounting rules for large companies are as follows.

6.25% p.a. from 18 February 2008
6.50% p.a. from 17 December 2007 to 17 February 2008
6.75% p.a. from 16 July 2007 to 16 December 2007
6.50% p.a. from 21 May 2007 to 15 July 2007
6.25% p.a. from 22 January 2007 to 20 May 2007

6.00% p.a. from 20 November 2006 to 21 January 2007
5.75% p.a. from 14 August 2006 to 19 November 2006

These rates apply up to the earlier of the date of payment and the normal due date (after which the normal rates apply).

Recent interest rates for accounting periods ending **before 1 July 1999** are as follows.

6.00% p.a. from 6 January 2008
6.75% p.a. from 6 August 2007 to 5 January 2008
6.00% p.a. from 6 September 2006 to 5 August 2007
5.25% p.a. from 6 September 2005 to 5 September 2006

40   Losses

40.6   **Anti-avoidance.** The fourth to seventh paragraphs are amended to read as follows.

'HMRC have published guidance on the operation of the provision. In their view, interdependence of transactions or of the terms on which transactions take place is a strong indicator (although not a necessary condition) of the existence of an arrangement. If, on the facts, any participant in arrangements is found to have a main purpose of achieving a tax advantage, that is considered to be sufficient to demonstrate that one of the main purposes of the arrangements is the securing of a tax advantage. HMRC is likely to examine carefully any relevant case in which a normal commercial objective is lacking, or where commercial objectives are not being sought in a straightforward manner. Where there is more than one way of achieving a commercial objective and a course of action is chosen on commercial grounds, any incidental tax advantage is not relevant. However, where the tax advantage was material to the choice the anti-avoidance legislation may be in point, but HMRC have indicated that this is unlikely to be the case unless there is evidence of additional, complex or costly steps included solely for tax reasons. Using a marketed tax avoidance scheme will be taken as an indicator that securing a tax advantage was a main purpose of the arrangements.

The guidance also includes 14 examples demonstrating how HMRC think the provision will operate in different circumstances.

(HMRC Guidance 'Avoidance through the creation and use of capital losses', 19 July 2007).

See also Taxation Magazine 19 April 2007, pp. 428–431 for comment on the draft version of HMRC's guidance (published on 21 March 2007).'

44   Offshore Settlements

44.19   **Transfers of value: attribution of gains to beneficiaries.** The case reference in the first paragraph is updated to *DP & Mrs B Herman v HMRC (Sp C 609), [2007] SSCD 571.*

45   Overseas Matters

45.1   **Introduction.** The third complete paragraph on page 580 is amended to read as follows.

'See **45.10** below for the special relief claimable where a UK business is transferred or divided between companies in different EC member states and **45.11** for the claim and double taxation relief available where a non-UK business is transferred or divided between companies in different EC member states. See **45.11A** below for relief on European cross-border mergers and **45.11B** below for the disapplication of these reliefs where a transparent entity is involved.'

45.9   **UK resident company transferring assets to overseas resident company.** The text following list item (ii) is replaced down to immediately before the heading 'Insurance companies' by the following.

'The following disposals are disregarded.

● For the purposes of (i) above, intra-group transfers within *TCGA 1992, s 171* (see **27.2** GROUPS OF COMPANIES). A charge will arise when a subsequent group company makes a disposal outside the group.

● For the purposes of (i) above, securities transferred by a transferor as part of the process of a merger to which *TCGA 1992, s 140E* applies (see **45.11A** below). In relation to a subsequent disposal of the shares or disposal by the transferee company of assets within (ii) above, the transferee is treated as if it were the transferor company.

● For the purposes of (i) above, securities transferred on or after 1 January 2007 by a transferor company as part of the process of the transfer of a business to which **45.10** or **45.11** below applies. In relation to a subsequent disposal of the securities or disposal by the transferee company of assets within (ii) above, the transferee is treated as if it were the transferor company.

● For the purposes of (ii) above, intra-group transfers which would be within *TCGA 1992, s 171* if for those purposes a group included (without qualification) non-UK resident companies. A charge will arise when a subsequent group company makes a disposal outside the group.

A claim under *TCGA 1992, s 140C* (transfer or division of non-UK business between different EC member states; see **45.11** below) precludes a claim under the above.

[*TCGA 1992, s 140, Sch 4 para 4(5); FA 2000, Sch 29 para 23; FA 2003, s 153(1)(b)(4); F(No 2)A 2005, s 64(2); SI 2007 No 3186, Sch 1 para 7, Sch 2 para 5*].

For interaction between (i) above and the exemptions relating to SUBSTANTIAL SHAREHOLDINGS OF COMPANIES, see **60.21**.'

45.10   **Transfer or division of UK business between companies in different EC member states.** The text is amended to read as follows.

'**Transfer of UK business.** A special relief may be claimed where a company resident in one EC member state transfers the whole or part of a business carried on by it in the UK to a company resident in another member state wholly in exchange for shares or debentures (for issues effected before 1 April 2005, securities (including shares)) in the latter company, provided that the further conditions below are satisfied.

For transfers before 1 January 2007, the relief could only be claimed in respect of a transfer of a trade, and both the transferor and transferee had to be a body incorporated under the law of a member state. For such transfers, it was specifically provided that a company was regarded as resident in a member state under the laws of which it was chargeable to tax because it was regarded as so resident (unless it was regarded under DOUBLE TAX RELIEF (**19.2**) arrangements entered into by the member state as resident in a territory not within any of the member states).

Division of UK business. The relief may also be claimed where a company resident in one EC member state transfers, on or after 1 January 2007, part of its business to one or more companies at least one of which is resident in another member state. The part of the transferor's business which is transferred must be carried on by the transferor in the UK and the transferor must continue to carry on a business after the transfer.

The transfer must be made in exchange for the issue of shares in or debentures of each transferee to the holders of shares in or debentures of the transferor, except where, and to the extent that, a transferee is prevented from meeting this requirement by reason only of *Companies Act 2006, s 658* (rule against limited company acquiring its own shares) or a corresponding provision in another member state.

The further conditions below must also be satisfied.

Further conditions. A claim for relief must be made by both the transferor and the transferee (or each of the transferees). The anti-avoidance provision below must not apply, and either:

(i)   if the transferee company is, or each of the transferee companies are, non-UK resident immediately after the transfer, any chargeable gain accruing to it, or them, on a disposal of the assets included in the transfer would form part of its, or their, corporation tax profits under *TCGA 1992, s 10(3)* or *s 10B*, or

(ii)   if it is or they are UK resident at that time, none of the assets included in the transfer is exempt from UK tax on disposal under double tax relief arrangements.

Effect of relief. Any assets included in the transfer are treated for the purposes of corporation tax on chargeable gains as transferred for a no gain/no loss consideration, and *TCGA 1992, s 25(3)* (deemed disposal by non-resident on ceasing to trade in the UK through a permanent establishment or a branch or agency, see **45.3** above) does not apply to the assets by reason of the transfer.

In the case of a division of a UK business, where the transfer is not made wholly in exchange for the issue of shares in or debentures of each transferee, neither *TCGA 1992, s 24* (deemed disposal where asset lost, destroyed or becoming of negligible value — see **15.3** COMPUTATION OF GAINS AND LOSSES and **40.9** LOSSES) nor *TCGA 1992, s 122* (capital distributions — see **58.10** SHARES AND SECURITIES) apply to the transfer.

Also in the case of a division of a UK business, where the transferor and transferee (or each of the transferees) are all resident in EU member states, but are not all resident in the same state, the transfer of assets is treated as if it were a scheme of reconstruction within *TCGA 1992, s 136* (see **58.6** SHARES AND SECURITIES) if it would not otherwise be so treated. Where *section 136* applies as a result of this provision, the anti-avoidance provision at *section 136(6)* does not apply (and neither does *section 137* (restrictions on company reconstructions — see **3.18** ANTI-AVOIDANCE)).

Anti-avoidance. The above provisions do not apply unless the transfer is effected for *bona fide* commercial reasons and not as part of a scheme or arrangement a main purpose of which is avoidance of income, corporation or capital gains taxes. Advance clearance may be obtained from HMRC on the application of the companies, to the same address and subject to the same conditions and appeal procedures as apply to clearances under *TCGA 1992, s 138* (see **3.18** ANTI-AVOIDANCE).

[*TCGA 1992, ss 140A, 140B, 140DA; FA 2003, Sch 27 para 2; F(No 2)A 2005, s 59(3)(7); FA 2007, s 110; SI 2007 No 3186, Sch 1 paras 2, 3, 6*].

The above provisions were introduced to comply with *EEC Directive No 90/434/EEC*. The changes applying on or after 1 January 2007 were made to comply with *Directive No 2005/19/EC*.

See also **55.7** ROLLOVER RELIEF.'

45.11   **Transfer or division of non-UK business between companies in different EC member states.** The text is replaced by the following.

'**Transfer of non-UK business.** Special provisions apply, on a claim, where a company resident in the UK transfers to a company resident in another member state the whole or part of a business carried on by the UK company immediately before the transfer through a permanent establishment (or, for accounting periods beginning before 1 January 2003, through a branch or agency) in a member state other than the UK. The transfer must be wholly or partly in exchange for shares or debentures (for issues effected before 1 April 2005, securities (including shares)) in the non-UK transferee company and the further conditions below must be satisfied.

For transfers before 1 January 2007, the provisions only applied in respect of a transfer of a trade, and both the transferor and transferee had to be a body incorporated under the law of a member state. For such transfers, it was specifically provided that a company was not regarded as resident in the UK if it were regarded under any DOUBLE TAX RELIEF (**19.2**) arrangements to which the UK was a party as resident in a territory not within any of the member states. A company was regarded as resident in another member state under the laws of which it was chargeable to tax because it was regarded as so resident (unless it was regarded under a double tax relief arrangement entered into by the member state as resident in a territory not within any of the member states).

Division of non-UK business. The provisions may also apply where a company resident in the UK transfers, on or after 1 January 2007, part of its business to one or more companies at least one of which is resident in another member state other than the UK. The part of the transferor's business which is transferred must be carried on by the transferor immediately before the transfer in a member state other than the UK through a permanent establishment and the transferor must continue to carry on a business after the transfer.

The transfer must be made in exchange for the issue of shares in or debentures of each transferee to the holders of shares in or debentures of the transferor, except where, and to the extent that, a transferee is prevented from meeting this requirement by reason only of *Companies Act 2006, s 658* (rule against limited company acquiring its own shares) or a corresponding provision in another member state.

The further conditions below must also be satisfied.

Further conditions. The transfer must include all the UK company's assets used in the business or part (with the possible exception of cash) and the anti-avoidance provision below must be satisfied. The aggregate of the chargeable gains accruing to the UK company on the transfer must exceed the aggregate of the allowable losses so accruing.

The UK company must make a claim for the provisions to apply. No claim may, however, be made where a claim is made under *TCGA 1992, s 140* at **45.9** above in relation to the same transfer.

Effect of provisions. The transfer is treated as giving rise to a single chargeable gain of the excess of the aggregate of the chargeable gains accruing to the UK company on the transfer over the aggregate of the allowable losses so accruing. As regards insurance companies, *ICTA 1988, s 442(3)* (also see **45.9** above) is ignored in arriving at the chargeable gains and allowable losses accruing on the transfer.

In the case of a division of a non-UK business, where the transferor and transferee (or each of the transferees) are all resident in EU member states, but are not all resident in the same state, the transfer of assets is treated as if it were a scheme of reconstruction within *TCGA 1992, s 136* (see **58.6** SHARES AND SECURITIES) if it would not otherwise be so treated. Where *section 136* applies as a result of this provision, the anti-avoidance provision at *section 136(6)* does not apply (and neither does *section 137* (restrictions on company reconstructions — see **3.18** ANTI-AVOIDANCE)).

Anti-avoidance. The transfer must be effected for *bona fide* commercial reasons and not as part of a scheme or arrangement a main purpose of which is avoidance of income, corporation or capital gains taxes. Advance clearance may be obtained from HMRC on the application of the UK company, to the same address and subject to the same conditions and appeal procedures as apply to clearances under *TCGA 1992, s 138* (see **3.18** ANTI-AVOIDANCE).

[*TCGA 1992, ss 140C, 140D, 140DA; FA 2003, s 153(1)(b)(4); F(No 2)A 2005, s 59(4)(7); FA 2007, s 110; SI 2007 No 3186, Sch 1 paras 4–6*].

The above provisions were introduced to comply with *EEC Directive No 90/434/EEC* (the 'Mergers Directive'). The changes applying on or after 1 January 2007 were made to comply with *Directive No 2005/19/EC*.

Double tax relief. Where the above provisions apply, where gains accruing to the UK company would have been chargeable to tax under the law of the member state in which the trade was carried on immediately before the transfer but for the Mergers Directive, the amount of tax is treated for double tax relief purposes as tax paid in that other member state. In calculating the amount of the tax so treated it is assumed that, so far as permitted under the law of the member state, any losses arising on the transfer are set against the gains, and that the UK company claims any available reliefs.

These provisions apply also where *TCGA 1992, s 140F* (European cross-border merger: assets not left within UK tax charge — see **45.11A** below) applies.

[*ICTA 1988, s 815A(3); FA 2003, s 153(1)(4); F(No 2)A 2005, s 59(1)*].'

45.11A   **European cross-border mergers.** The following new section is added.

'The following provisions were originally introduced to facilitate the tax-neutral formation of SEs (see **13.18** COMPANIES) by merger, but have since been extended to apply also to the formation of SCEs (see **13.19** COMPANIES) by merger and other mergers of companies resident in different EU member states. Accordingly, the provisions apply to:

(*a*)   the formation of an SE on or after 1 April 2005 by the merger of two or more companies in accordance with *Council Regulation (EC) No 2157/2001, Arts 2(1), 17(2)*;

(*b*)   the formation of an SCE on or after 18 August 2006 by the merger of two or more 'co-operative societies', at least one of which is a society registered under *Industrial and Provident Societies Act 1965*, in accordance with *Council Regulation (EC) No 1435/2003*;

(*c*)   a merger on or after 1 January 2007 effected by the transfer by one or more companies or co-operative societies of all their assets and liabilities to a single existing company or co-operative society; and

(*d*)   a merger on or after 1 January 2007 effected by the transfer by two or more companies of all their assets to a single new company (which is not an SE or SCE) in exchange for the issue by the transferee company of shares or debentures to each person holding shares in or debentures of a transferee company.

For the purposes of (*b*) and (*c*) above, a '*co-operative society*' is a society registered under the *Industrial and Provident Societies Act 1965* or a similar society established under the law of a member state other than the UK.

Each of the merging companies or co-operative societies must be resident in a member state but they must not all be resident in the same state. For mergers before 18 August 2006, it was specifically provided that a company was resident in a member state for this purpose if it was within a charge to tax under the law of the State as being resident for that purpose and it was not regarded, for the purposes of any DOUBLE TAX RELIEF (**19**) arrangements to which the state was a party, as resident in a territory not within a member state.

Treatment of securities issued on merger. If it does not constitute or form part of a scheme of reconstruction within the meaning of *TCGA 1992, s 136* (see **58.6** SHARES AND SECURITIES), the merger is nevertheless treated as if it were a scheme of reconstruction for the purposes of that section, but the anti-avoidance provision at *section 136(6)* does not apply (and neither does *section 137* (restrictions on company reconstructions — see **3.18** ANTI-AVOIDANCE)). See, however, the anti-avoidance provision below.

Assets left within UK tax charge. If:

(i)   *TCGA 1992, s 139* (reconstruction involving transfer of business — see **13.10** COMPA-NIES) does not apply to the merger;

(ii)   where the merger is within (*b*) or (*c*) above, or is within (*a*) above and takes place on or after 18 August 2006, the transfer of assets and liabilities is made in exchange for the issue of shares in or debentures of the transferee to the holders of shares in or debentures of a transferor, except where, and to the extent that, the transferee is prevented from meeting this requirement by reason only of *Companies Act 2006, s 658* (rule against limited company acquiring its own shares) or a corresponding provision in another member state; and

(iii)   where the merger is within (*d*) above, in the course of the merger each transferor ceases to exist without being in liquidation (within the meaning of *Insolvency Act 1986, s 247*),

then any 'qualifying transferred assets' are treated for chargeable gains purposes as acquired by the transferee (i.e. the SE, SCE or merged company) for a consideration resulting in neither gain nor loss for the transferor company or co-operative society.

For this purpose, an asset transferred to the transferee as part of the merger process is a '*qualifying transferred asset*' if

●   either the transferor was resident in the UK at the time of the transfer or any gain accruing on disposal of the asset immediately before that time would have been a chargeable gain forming part of the transferor's chargeable profits by virtue of *TCGA 1992, s 10B* (trade carried on via UK permanent establishment — see **45.3** above); and

●   either the transferee is resident in the UK at the time of the transfer or any gain accruing to it on disposal of the asset immediately after the transfer would have been a chargeable gain forming part of its chargeable profits by virtue of *TCGA 1992, s 10B*.

Where the condition at (ii) above applies, but the transfer is not made wholly in exchange for the issue of shares in or debentures of each transferee, neither *TCGA 1992, s 24* (deemed disposal where asset lost, destroyed or becoming of negligible value — see **15.3** COMPUTATION OF GAINS AND LOSSES and **40.9** LOSSES) nor *TCGA 1992, s 122* (capital distributions — see **58.10** SHARES AND SECURITIES) apply to the transfer.

Assets not left within UK tax charge. If

●   in the course of the merger a company or co-operative society resident in the UK (company A) transfers to a company or co-operative society resident in another member state all the assets and liabilities relating to a business carried on by company A in a member state other than the UK through a permanent establishment;

●   the aggregate chargeable gains accruing to company A on the transfer exceed the aggregate allowable losses; and

●   where the merger is within (*b*) or (*c*) above, or is within (*a*) above and takes place on or after 18 August 2006, the transfer of assets and liabilities is made in exchange for the issue of shares in or debentures of the transferee to the holders of shares in or debentures of a transferor, except where, and to the extent that, the transferee is prevented from meeting this requirement by reason only of *Companies Act 2006, s 658* (rule against limited company acquiring its own shares) or a corresponding provision in another member state,

the allowable losses are treated as set off against the chargeable gains and the transfer is treated as giving rise to a single chargeable gain equal to the excess. See **45.11** above for special double tax relief provisions applying where this provision applies.

Anti-avoidance. The above provisions do not apply if the merger is not effected for *bona fide* commercial reasons or if it forms part of a scheme or arrangements of which the main purpose, or one of the main purposes, is avoiding liability to UK tax. The advance clearance provisions of *TCGA 1992, s 138* (see **3.18** ANTI-AVOIDANCE) apply, with any necessary modifications, for this purpose as they apply for the purposes of *TCGA 1992, s 137*.

[*TCGA 1992, ss 140E–140G; F(No 2)A 2005, s 51; FA 2007, s 110; SI 2007 No 3186, Sch 2 para 2*].

Held-over gains. For the effect of a cross-border merger on various hold-over reliefs, see **45.9** above, **50.3** QUALIFYING CORPORATE BONDS and **55.7** ROLLOVER RELIEF.'

45.11B **Transparent entities: disapplication of reliefs.** The following new section is added.

'The following provisions operate to disapply certain of the tax reliefs enacted to comply with the European Mergers Directive (*EEC Directive No 90/434/EEC*) where one of the parties to the transaction is a 'transparent entity'. In some cases, the disapplication of the reliefs is accompanied by a notional tax credit for the shareholder or interest holder in the transparent entity. The provisions apply in relation to mergers relating to the formation of an SE (see **13.18** COMPANIES) or SCE (see **13.19** COMPANIES) which take place on or after 18 August 2006 and in relation to all other mergers which take place on or after 1 January 2007. [*SI 2007 No 3186, Reg 3(3)*].

A '*transparent entity*' for this purpose is an entity resident in a member state other than the UK which is listed as a company in the Annex to the Mergers Directive but which does not have an 'ordinary share capital' (within *ICTA 1988, s 832*) and, if it were UK-resident, would not be capable of being a company within the meaning of *Companies Act 2006*.

Except where the context requires otherwise, a 'company' is, for the purposes of the provisions, an entity listed as a company in the Annex to the Mergers Directive. A company is regarded as resident in another member state under the laws of which it is chargeable to tax because it is regarded as so resident (unless it is regarded under a double tax relief arrangement entered into by the member state as resident in a territory not within any of the member states).

[*TCGA 1992, s 140L; SI 2007 No 3186, Sch 3 para 1*].

Share exchanges. Where a company (company B) issues shares or debentures to a person in exchange for shares in or debentures of another company (company A) and either of the companies is a transparent entity, the share exchange provisions at *TCGA 1992, s 135* (see **58.4** SHARES AND SECURITIES) are disapplied.

Where the exchange otherwise meets the conditions for *TCGA 1992, s 135* to apply, any tax which would, but for the Mergers Directive, have been chargeable on a gain accruing to a holder of shares in or debentures of company A on the exchange under the law of a member state other than the UK is treated, for the purposes of DOUBLE TAX RELIEF (**19**), as if it had been so chargeable. This notional tax is calculated on the basis that, so far as permitted under the law of the relevant member state, losses arising on the exchange are set against gains arising from the exchange and that any relief available to company A under that law has been claimed.

[*TCGA 1992, s 140H; SI 2007 No 3186, Sch 3 para 1*].

Division of business or transfer of assets. Where:

● there is a transfer of a business, or part of a business, to which *TCGA 1992, s 140A* (see **45.10** above) applies (or would apply if the business or part transferred were carried on by the transferor in the UK and either **45.10**(i) or (ii) above were satisfied in relation to the transferee or each of the transferees), and

● either the transferor or transferee, or one of the transferees, is a transparent entity,

then, if the transferor is the transparent entity, neither *section 140A* nor *TCGA 1992, s 140DA* (transfer of assets treated as scheme of reconstruction — see **45.10** above) apply to the transfer. If a transferee is the transparent entity, *section 140DA* does not apply to the transfer to it.

Any tax which would, but for the Mergers Directive, have been chargeable on a 'transfer gain' under the law of a member state other than the UK is treated, for the purposes of DOUBLE TAX RELIEF (**19**), as if it had been so chargeable. This notional tax is calculated on the basis that, so far as permitted under the law of the relevant member state, losses arising on the transfer are set against gains arising from the transfer and that any relief available under that law has been claimed. A '*transfer gain*' for this purpose is a gain accruing to a transparent entity (or which would be treated as accruing to such an entity were it not transparent) by reason of the transfer of assets by the transparent entity to the transferee.

[*TCGA 1992, s 140I; SI 2007 No 3186, Sch 3 para 1*].

Cross-border merger. Where there is a merger within **45.11A**(*a*)–(*d*) above which meets the conditions at **45.11A**(i)–(iii) and one or more of the merging companies is a transparent entity:

● if the assets and liabilities of a transparent entity are transferred to another company on the merger, *TCGA 1992, s 140E* (assets left within charge to UK tax — see **45.11A** above) and *TCGA 1992, s 140G* (treatment of securities issued on merger — see **45.11A** above) do not apply; and

● if the assets and liabilities of one or more companies are transferred to a transparent entity on the merger, *TCGA 1992, s 140G* does not apply.

Any tax which would, but for the Mergers Directive, have been chargeable on a 'merger gain' under the law of a member state other than the UK is treated, for the purposes of DOUBLE TAX RELIEF (**19**), as if it had been so chargeable. This notional tax is calculated on the basis that, so far as permitted under the law of the relevant member state, losses arising on the merger are set against gains arising from the merger and that any relief available under that law has been claimed. A '*merger gain*' for this purpose is a gain accruing to a transparent entity (or which would be treated as accruing to such an entity were it not transparent) by reason of the transfer of assets by the transparent entity on the merger.

[*TCGA 1992, s 140J; SI 2007 No 3186, Sch 3 para 1*].

Taxation of transparent entity after merger or division. Where

(i) a transparent entity (company A) is a transferee for the purposes of *TCGA 1992, s 140A(1A)* (division of UK business — see **45.10** above) or *TCGA 1992, s 140E* (cross-border merger: assets left within charge to UK tax — see **45.11A** above);

(ii) a person ('X') with an interest in company A was or is also a shareholder or debenture holder of a company (company B);

(iii) X became entitled to an interest, or an increased interest, in company A in exchange for a disposal of share in, or debenture of, company B on a merger to which *TCGA 1992, s 140E* applied or on a transfer to which *TCGA 1992, s 140(1A)* applied;

(iv) a chargeable gain accrued to X on the disposal of shares or debentures of company B;

(v) in calculating that gain account was taken of the value of an asset of company B; and

(vi) X makes a disposal of his interest in the asset,

then, in calculating the gain on the disposal in (vi) above, the amount allowed as the acquisition cost in relation to the interest, or proportion of the interest, which X acquired on the merger or transfer is the amount to be taken into account in computing the gain on the disposal of his shares in, or debentures of, company B.

References above to an interest in company A include an interest in the assets of, or shares in or debentures of, company A.

[*TCGA 1992, s 140K; SI 2007 No 3186, Sch 3 para 1*].'

46   Partnerships

46.3   The last sentence of the first paragraph is amended to read as follows.

'The Statements of Practice are supplemented by the HMRC Capital Gains Manual at CG 27000–27902 and HMRC Brief 3/2008.'

46.5A   A new section is inserted as follows.

'**Contribution of assets to a partnership.** Where an asset is transferred to a partnership by means of a capital contribution by a partner, HMRC consider that the partner makes a part disposal of the asset equal to the fractional share that passes to the other partners. Where the market value rule does not apply, the consideration for the disposal is a proportion of the total consideration given by the partnership for the asset. The proportion is equal to the fractional share of the asset passing to the other partners. HMRC consider that a sum credited to the partner's capital account represents consideration for this purpose. Allowable costs are apportioned on a fractional basis as in **46.6** below.

Where, before the publication of HMRC Brief 3/2008, individual HMRC officers sought incorrectly to apply the principles at 46.6 below to the contribution of an asset to a partnership, HMRC accept that they are bound by the statements made by the officer.

(HMRC Brief 3/2008).'

47   Payment of Tax

47.8   **Recovery of foreign taxes etc.** The following paragraph is added at the end.

'**Tax enforcement agreements.** Provision is made for the Treasury to make regulations for the recovery in the UK of foreign taxes covered by a tax enforcement agreement with another country (see **29.2**(*c*) HMRC: CONFIDENTIALITY OF INFORMATION). See now *SI 2007 No 3507*. [*FA 2006, s 175*].'

48   Penalties

48.6   **Negligence or fraud in connection with return or accounts.** The first paragraph is amended to read as follows.

'**Capital gains tax (and income tax).** The following provisions are repealed and replaced by the provisions at **48.10** below with effect for returns and accounts relating to 2008/09 onwards. [*FA 2007, s 97, Sch 24 para 29; SI 2008 No 568*].'

48.7   **Partnerships.** The first paragraph is amended to read as follows.

'Provisions similar to those at **48.6** above apply as regards partnership returns under *TMA 1970, s 12AA* (see **54.15** RETURNS). They are likewise repealed and replaced by the provisions at **48.10** below with effect for returns and accounts relating to 2008/09 onwards. [*FA 2007, s 97, Sch 24 para 29; SI 2008 No 568*].'

48.8   **Companies.** The first paragraph is amended to read as follows.

'The following provisions are repealed and replaced by the provisions at **48.10** below with effect for returns and accounts relating to accounting periods beginning on or after 1 April 2008. [*FA 2007, s 97, Sch 24 para 29; SI 2008 No 568*].'

48.10   **Careless or deliberate errors in documents.** The first paragraph is amended to read as follows.

'The following provisions apply for the purposes of capital gains tax and corporation tax on chargeable gains to documents relating to tax years and accounting periods beginning on or after 1 April 2008 and replace those at **48.6–48.8** above. No penalty can be charged under the provisions in respect of a tax year or accounting period for which a return is required before 1 April 2009.'

A reference to *SI 2008 No 568* is added to the list of statutory instruments at the end.

48.11   **Failure to notify HMRC of error in assessment.** The first paragraph is amended to read as follows.

'In relation to assessments for tax years or accounting periods beginning on or after 1 April 2008, a penalty is payable by a person if an assessment issued to him by HMRC understates his liability to tax and he or a person acting on his behalf has failed to take reasonable steps to notify HMRC of the under-assessment, within the 30 days beginning with the date of the assessment.'

A reference to *SI 2008 No 568* is added to the list of statutory instruments at the end.

48.18   **Failure to disclose tax avoidance scheme.** The following replaces the second paragraph.

'Higher maximum continuing daily penalties of up to £5,000 apply where

(*a*)   an order has been made under *FA 2004, s 306A* (order by Special Commissioners to treat proposal or arrangements as notifiable); or

(*b*)   there is a failure to comply with an order made under *FA 2004, s 314A* (order by the Special Commissioners to make a disclosure).

In the case of (*b*) above, however, the increased maximum only applies to days falling after the period of ten days beginning with the date of the order.

Where an order to disclose is made under *FA 2004, s 314A*, the person mentioned in the order cannot rely on doubt as to notifiability as a reasonable excuse after the period of ten days beginning with the date of the order and any delay in compliance after that time is unreasonable unless there is another excuse.'

49   Private Residences

49.6   **Occupation by dependent relative.** The final paragraph is amended to read as follows.

'Where a property qualifies for the main private residence exemption only by virtue of these provisions, HMRC accept that the residential lettings exemption at **49.8** below may be available. (HMRC Capital Gains Manual CG 64718). Note that this represents a change of view by HMRC, who, before August 2007 took the opposite view that the exemption was not available in such circumstances. See HMRC Internet Statement 1 August 2007.'

50   Qualifying Corporate Bonds

50.2   **Definition of corporate bond.** The following is added to (*b*).

'Securities carrying an option for redemption in a foreign currency do not become corporate bonds when the option lapses (*Harding v HMR, Ch D [2008] EWHC 99 (Ch), 2008 STI 221*).'

51   Remittance Basis

51.1   **General.** The following paragraph is added at the end.

'*Proposed changes to remittance basis.* The 2008 Finance Bill is to include provisions which will allow non-domiciled individuals who have been resident in the UK for seven years to use the remittance basis only if they pay an additional tax charge of £30,000. The provisions will apply for 2008/09 onwards, and all previous years of residence will count towards the seven-year total. The details of the provisions, and of further changes to remove certain anomalies from the remittance basis rules, are subject to consultation. (2007 Pre-Budget Report Notice 18, 9 October 2007).'

52   Residence and Domicile

52.3   **Residence.** The third paragraph at (*b*) is amended to read as follows.

'In applying the 91-day test above, days of arrival in and departure from the UK are normally disregarded. In *Gaines-Cooper v HMRC Ch D, [2007] EWHC 2617 (Ch), 2007 STI 2651*, however, HMRC successfully argued before the Special Commissioners that, in the particular circumstances of the case, disregarding those days produced a distorted picture of the taxpayer's presence in the UK and therefore days of arrival and departure should not be disregarded. The Ch D upheld the Special Commissioners' decision. Following the decision in this case, HMRC have indicated that they consider the 91-day test to apply only where the taxpayer has left the UK (which the appellant in that case had not). HMRC continue normally to disregard days of arrival and departure where they are satisfied that an individual has left the UK. (HMRC Brief 1/2007). The Government has announced, however, that for 2008/09 onwards, days of arrival and departure are to be counted as days of presence in the UK (2007 Pre-Budget Report Notice 18, 9 October 2007).'

52.5   **Visits abroad and claims to non-UK residence and to non-UK ordinary residence.** The final sentence is amended to read as follows.

'See also *Gaines-Cooper v HMRC* at **52.3**(*b*) above and *Grace v HMRC (Sp C 663), 2008 STI 279*.'

52.6   **Companies.** The final paragraph is amended to read as follows.

'**European Companies (SEs) and European Co-operatives (SCEs).** An SE (a European Company — see **13.18** COMPANIES) which transfers its registered office to the UK on or after 1 April 2005 in accordance with *Council Regulation (EC) 2157/2001, Art 8* is regarded upon registration in the UK as resident in the UK for tax purposes. If a different place of residence is given by any rule of law, that place is not taken into account for tax purposes. Where this rule applies, the SE is not treated as ceasing to be UK-resident by reason only of the subsequent transfer from the UK of its registered office. These rules apply also to an SCE (a European Co-operative — see **13.19** COMPANIES) which transfers its registered office to the UK on or after 18 August 2006 in accordance with *Council Regulation (EC) 1435/2003, Art 7*. [*FA 1988, s 66A; F(No 2)A 2005, s 60(1)(3); SI 2007 No 3186, Sch 2 para 15*]. This provision is subject to *FA 1994, s 249* above.'

52.7   **Domicile.** The final case reference in the third paragraph is updated to *Gaines-Cooper v HMRC Ch D, [2007] EWHC 2617 (Ch), 2007 STI 2651*.

54   Returns

54.2   **Annual tax returns.** The following paragraph is added immediately before the heading 'Reporting limits'.

'Following a breakdown in HMRC's online return service on 31 January 2008, HMRC have accepted that returns for 2006/07 received by midnight on 1 February 2008 are to be treated as filed on time. Where users were unable to file a return by midnight on 1 February 2008 due to problems with the service on 31 January or 1 February, HMRC will accept a reasonable excuse and remove any late filing penalty and treat the return as filed on time, provided that the return is filed within a reasonable period. In addition, HMRC have stopped the issue of penalty notices, and the extension of the enquiry window, for online returns filed using HMRC software on 2 and 3 February 2008 and for paper returns received in local offices by close of business on 4 February 2008. They will accept appeals against penalties issued in respect of online returns filed within a reasonable period on or after 4 February 2008 and for paper returns filed on or after 5 February or later where the delay was due to problems with the online service. (HMRC Notice, 18 February 2008).'

54.3   **Form and delivery of returns.** The paragraph headed 'Substitute returns' is amended to read as follows.

'*Substitute returns.* HMRC have issued a Statement of Practice (HMRC SP 5/87) concerning the acceptability of facsimile and photocopied tax returns. Whenever such a substitute form is used, it is important to ensure that it bears the correct taxpayer's reference. For 2007/08 returns onwards, HMRC will not accept computer generated substitute individual, partnership or trust returns (HMRC Internet Statement 25 October 2007).'

54.9   **Conduct of enquiry.** The text is amended to read as follows.

'A Code of Practice (COP 11 for individuals etc., COP 14 for companies, or in certain simple cases a short, single-page version of whichever is relevant) will be issued at the start of every enquiry. This sets out the rules under which enquiries are made into returns and explains how taxpayers can expect HMRC to conduct enquiries. It describes what HMRC do when they receive a return and how they select cases for enquiry, how they open and carry out enquiries, and what happens if they find something wrong.

HMRC have also published an Enquiry Manual as part of their series of internal guidance manuals (see **30.2** HMRC EXPLANATORY PUBLICATIONS) and, as an extended introduction to the material on operational aspects of the enquiry regime covered in the manual, a special edition of their Tax Bulletin (Special Edition 2, August 1997). The following points are selected from the Bulletin.

- Early submission of a tax return will not increase the likelihood of selection for enquiry.

- HMRC do not have to give reasons for opening an enquiry — and they *will not do so* (but see further below).

- Enquiries may be full enquiries or 'aspect enquiries'. An aspect enquiry will fall short of an in-depth examination of the return (though it may develop into one), but will instead concentrate on one or more aspects of it.

- Greater emphasis than before is placed on examination of underlying records. HMRC will make an informal request for information before, if necessary, using their powers under *TMA 1970, s 19A* (see **54.10** below).

- Where penalties are being sought, HMRC will aim to conclude the enquiry by means of a contract settlement (as was the case with pre-self-assessment investigations — see **23.12** FRAUDULENT OR NEGLIGENT CONDUCT) rather than issue a closure notice under *TMA 1970, s 28A* (see **54.11** below).

In October 2007, HMRC announced that they intend to test new approaches to enquiries over the period November 2007 to April 2008. Under the 'openness' approach, HMRC will advise the taxpayer whether the enquiry is a full or aspect enquiry and *why the enquiry has been opened.* Under the 'early dialogue' approach, HMRC will aim to agree with the taxpayer and their agent an explicit timetable for an initial meeting (or telephone conversation), the production of information and documents, records examination, and discussion of findings. (HMRC Internet Statement, 29 October 2007).

Where an enquiry remains open beyond the period during which notice of intention to enquire had to be given (see above) and solely because of an unagreed valuation for capital gains tax purposes, HMRC will not take advantage of the open enquiry to raise further enquiries into matters unrelated to the valuation or the CGT computation except in circumstances where a 'discovery' (see **5.2** ASSESSMENTS) could in any case have been made if the enquiry had been completed (HMRC Statement of Practice 1/99).

See also HMRC Pamphlet IR 160 (Inland Revenue Enquiries under Self-Assessment).'

54.10 **Power to call for documents.** The following paragraph is added immediately before the final paragraph.

'The Appeal Commissioners cannot set aside a notice under *TMA 1970, s 19A* on the grounds of the taxpayer's ill health (*Mr A v HMRC (Sp C 650), 2008 STI 27*).'

55 Rollover Relief — Replacement of Business Assets

55.7 **Wasting assets.** The third, fourth and fifth paragraphs are amended to read as follows.

'A transfer of the new asset or of shares in a company which holds the new asset as part of the process of a cross-border merger to which *TCGA 1992,s 140E* (European cross-border mergers: assets left within UK charge to tax — see **45.11A** OVERSEAS MATTERS) applies does not bring the held-over gain into charge under the above provisions. In such circumstances, if the transferee holds the new asset it is treated as if it had claimed the rollover relief. If the transferee holds shares in the company which holds the new asset, *TCGA 1992, s 175* (see **55.5** above) applies as if the transferee's group were the same group as any group of which the company claiming the rollover relief was a member before the merger. [*TCGA 1992, s 154(2A)(2C); F(No 2)A 2005, s 64(3); SI 2007 No 3186, Sch 2 para 6*].

Where, as part of the process of a cross-border merger to which *TCGA 1992, s 140E* applies, the transferee becomes a member of a group of which a company which has claimed rollover relief in respect of a wasting asset is a member, *TCGA 1992, s 175* (see **55.5** above) applies for the purposes of determining when the held-over gain is brought into charge as if the group of which the transferee is a member were the same group as the group of which the claimant was a member before the merger. [*TCGA 1992, s 154(2B)(2C); F(No 2)A 2005, s 64(3); SI 2007 No 3186, Sch 2 para 6*].

The above cross-border merger provisions apply also to the transfer of an asset on or after 1 January 2007 in circumstances where *TCGA 1992, s 140A* (transfer or division of UK business between companies in different EC member states — see **45.10** OVERSEAS MATTERS) applies (with references to a merger being treated as references to the transfer). [*TCGA 1992, s 154(2D); SI 2007 No 3186, Sch 1 para 8*].'

56 Self-Assessment

56.4 **Interim payments of tax on account.** The following paragraph is added immediately before the first complete paragraph on page 740.

'The de minimis limit in (*c*) above is to be increased from £500 to £1,000 for the purposes of income tax due for 2009/10 onwards (2007 Pre-Budget Notice 28, 9 October 2007).'

57 Settlements

57.8 **Sub-fund settlements.** The following paragraph is added at the end.

'HMRC accept that where the transaction creating the sub-fund settlement is a chargeable transfer for inheritance tax purposes and it takes place on the day the election takes effect, the deemed disposal will qualify for relief under *TCGA 1992, s 260* (see **33.7** HOLD-OVER RELIEFS). (HMRC Capital Gains Manual, CG 33331).'

58 Shares and securities

58.4 **Exchange of securities for those in another company.** The following is added to the end of the second paragraph.

'For HMRC's interpretation of 'ordinary share capital', see HMRC Brief 54/2007.'

58.6 **'Scheme of reconstruction' involving issue of securities.** The following paragraph is added immediately before the example.

'*Cross-border divisions and mergers.* Certain transfers of assets on the division of a business between companies in different EC member states and certain transfers of assets and liabilities on cross-border mergers are treated as schemes of reconstruction. See **45.10–45.11A** OVERSEAS MATTERS.'

58.22 **Agreements for sale and repurchase of securities ('repos').** The text from the beginning to immediately before the heading 'Gain accruing to person paying manufactured dividend' on page 805 is replaced by the following.

'There are special income tax and corporation tax provisions dealing with agreements for sale and repurchase of securities (commonly known as 'repos'). Such an agreement involves one party agreeing to sell securities (typically these would be corporate bonds, gilts or other Government securities or shares) to another, with a related agreement (either a forward contract or an option) to buy back the securities at an agreed date and price. Broadly, any difference between the sale and repurchase price is treated for the purposes of tax on income as interest, and the sale and repurchase are ignored for the purposes of tax on chargeable gains. With effect for agreements coming into force on or after 1 October 2007, there are separate rules for corporation tax purposes, based on accounting principles. The pre-existing rules continue to apply for income tax and capital gains tax purposes. See Tolley's Income Tax and Tolley's Corporation Tax under Anti-Avoidance for the detailed income provisions. The chargeable gains provisions are detailed below.

Corporation tax on chargeable gains (agreements coming into force on or after 1 October 2007). *Debtor repos.* Where a company (the '*borrower*') has a 'debtor repo' and, having sold the securities under the repo arrangement to another party (the '*lender*'), is the only person with the right or obligation under the arrangement to repurchase those or similar securities, the sale and repurchase are ignored for the purposes of corporation tax on chargeable gains.

Where, however, at any time after the initial sale, it becomes apparent that the borrower will not make the repurchase or the accounting condition below ceases to be met, the borrower is treated for chargeable gains purposes as disposing of the securities at that time at market value. If the borrower does in fact subsequently make the repurchase this is not then ignored under the above provision.

The accounting condition mentioned above ceases to be met if, under generally accepted accounting practice, the borrower's accounts for any period after the one in which the 'advance' (i.e. the money or other asset received from the lender) is made do not record a financial liability in respect of the advance (except as a result of the subsequent purchase of the securities or similar securities).

For this purpose, a '*debtor repo*' is defined in *FA 2007, Sch 13 para 2* as, broadly, a repo from the point of view of the company selling and repurchasing the securities. References above to the borrower include a partnership of which the borrower is a member.

[*FA 2007, s 47, Sch 13 para 6*].

Creditor repos. Similarly, where a company (the '*lender*') has a 'creditor repo' and, having bought the securities under the repo arrangement from another party (the '*borrower*'), is the only person with the right or obligation under the arrangement to sell those or similar securities, the purchase and sale under the arrangement are ignored for the purposes of corporation tax on chargeable gains.

Where, however, at any time after the initial sale, it becomes apparent that the lender will not make the sale under the agreement or the accounting condition below ceases to be met, the lender is treated for chargeable gains purposes as acquiring the securities at that time at market value. If the seller does in fact subsequently make the sale this is not then ignored under the above provision.

The accounting condition ceases to be met if, under generally accepted accounting practice, the lender's accounts for any period after the one in which the 'advance' (i.e. the money or other asset received by the lender) is made do not record a financial asset in respect of the advance (except as a result of the subsequent sale of the securities or similar securities).

For this purpose, a '*creditor repo*' is defined in *FA 2007, Sch 13 para 7* as, broadly, a repo from the point of view of the company buying and then selling the securities. References above to the lender include a partnership of which the lender is a member.

[*FA 2007, s 47, Sch 13 para 11*].

Redemption arrangements. The above provisions apply with modifications in cases involving 'redemption arrangements'. For this purpose, a case involves '*redemption arrangements*' where arrangements, corresponding to those in repo cases, are made in relation to securities that are to be redeemed in the period after the sale, and a person, instead of having the right or obligation to buy back those or other securities, has a right or obligation in respect of the benefits that will result from the redemption. The definitions of 'debtor repo' and 'creditor repo' are modified to include such arrangements, and for chargeable gains purposes, the company selling the securities under the arrangement is treated as disposing of the securities when the redemption takes place, and the company buying the securities is treated as acquiring them at that time, for an amount equivalent to the redemption proceeds. [*FA 2007, Sch 13 para 15(6); SI 2007 No 2485, Regs 3, 4*].

Treasury power to amend provisions. The Treasury may, by regulations, modify the above provisions in relation to certain non-standard repos and cases involving redemption arrangements. This may include modification of *TCGA 1992* in relation to cases where, as a result of the regulations, an acquisition or disposal is excluded from those ignored for chargeable gains purposes under the above provisions. Regulations have been made in respect of redemption arrangements (see above) and non-standard repos involving the substitution of securities. [*FA 2007, Sch 13 para 15; SI 2007 No 2485*].

Capital gains tax (and corporation tax on chargeable gains before the *FA 2007* provisions take effect). Where *ITA 2007, s 607(1)* or *ICTA 1988, s 730A(1)* apply to treat the price differential on sale and repurchase as an interest payment (or where *ICTA 1988, s 730A(1)* would apply were the sale and repurchase price different), the acquisition and disposal by the interim holder, and (except where the repurchaser is or may be different from the original owner) the disposal and acquisition (as repurchaser) by the original owner, are disregarded for chargeable gains purposes. This does not, however, apply

(a)   (before the introduction of the *FA 2007* corporation tax provisions) where the repurchase price falls to be computed by reference to the provisions of *ICTA 1988, s 737C* ('manufactured' dividends and interest; see Tolley's Income Tax or Tolley's Corporation Tax under Anti-Avoidance) which are not in force in relation to the securities when the repurchase price becomes due; or

(b)   if the agreement(s) in question are non-arm's length agreements, or if all the benefits or risks arising from fluctuations in the market value of the securities accrue to, or fall on, the interim holder; or

(c)   in relation to any disposal or acquisition of QUALIFYING CORPORATE BONDS (**50**) where the securities disposed of by the original owner, or those acquired by him or another person as repurchaser, are not such bonds.

Where, however, at any time following the introduction of the *FA 2007* corporation tax provisions and after the initial sale, it becomes apparent that the interim holder will not dispose of the securities to the repurchaser, he is treated for capital gains tax purposes as acquiring the securities at that time at market value. Similarly, where at any time (after the introduction of the *FA 2007* corporation tax provisions) it becomes apparent that the original owner will not acquire the securities as repurchaser, he is treated for capital gains tax purposes as disposing of the securities at that time at market value.

In a case involving 'redemption arrangements' (defined, broadly as above, at *ITA 2007, s 613(2)*) where the transfer of securities takes place on or after 1 October 2007, the original owner is treated as disposing of the securities when the redemption takes place, and the interim holder is treated as acquiring them at that time, for an amount equivalent to the redemption proceeds.

[*TCGA 1992, s 263A; ITA 2007, Sch 1 para 334; FA 2007, Sch 14 para 12; SI 2007 No 2486, Regs 3, 4*].

Where *ITA 2007, s 607* or *ICTA 1988, s 730A(1)* apply but *TCGA 1992, s 263A* does not, the repurchase price is, as the case may be, either reduced by the excess of that price over the sale price or increased by the excess of the sale price over that price for chargeable gains purposes. [*TCGA 1992, s 261G; ICTA 1988, s 730A(2)(4); ITA 2007, Sch 1 paras 164, 331, 332*].

Where the repurchase price falls to be computed by reference to the provisions of *ITA 2007, s 604* (deemed increase in repurchase price: price differences under repos) or *ICTA 1988, s 737C* and *TCGA 1992, s 263A* does not apply, the deemed increase in that price also has effect for chargeable gains purposes. For capital gains tax purposes, where *ITA 2007, s 604* applies, either there must be no difference for the purposes of *ITA 2007, s 607* between the sale and repurchase price as a result of the increase, or that section must not apply as a result of an exemption in *ITA 2007, s 608*. [*TCGA 1992, s 261F; ICTA 1988, s 737C(11A); ITA 2007, Sch 1 para 330*].'

58.24   **Recognised stock exchanges**. The following is added to the end of the third paragraph.

'Certain exchanges have been designated as recognised stock exchanges for the purposes only of *FA 2005, s 48A* (see **15.9** COMPUTATION OF GAINS AND LOSSES). See HMRC's Order, 20 July 2007.'

---

59   Shares and Securities — Identification Rules

59.1   **Introduction.** The following is added at the end.

'**Proposed revised identification rules after 5 April 2008.** The Government intends to introduce simplified identification rules for capital gains tax purposes for disposals on or after 6 April 2008. The changes will be made possible as a result of the reforms proposed in the 2007 Pre-Budget Report (see **1.1A** INTRODUCTION), and will not apply for the purposes of corporation tax on chargeable gains. The rules will identify disposals with acquisitions in the following order.

- acquisitions on the same day as the disposal;

- acquisitions within 30 days after the day of disposal;

- shares comprised in a single pool incorporating all other shares of the same class, whenever acquired (thus including both the section 104 holding and the 1982 holding).

(2007 Pre-Budget Report Notice 17, 9 October 2007).'

---

61   Taper Relief

61.1   **Introduction.** The following paragraph is added at the end.

'The Government has announced that taper relief is to be withdrawn for disposals and deferred gains coming into charge on or after 6 April 2008 (2007 Pre-Budget Report Notice 17, 9 October 2007).'

---

65   Unit Trusts and Other Investment Vehicles

65.3   **Investment trusts.** The following is added to the fourth paragraph from the end.

'For HMRC's interpretation of 'ordinary share capital', see HMRC Brief 54/2007.'

65.4   **Real estate investment trusts.** The first paragraph is amended to read as follows.

'For accounting periods beginning on or after 1 January 2007, companies meeting the necessary conditions (see below) can elect to become real estate investment trusts. The 'property rental business' (as defined, and including both UK and overseas property) of such a trust is ring-fenced and treated as if it were a separate business carried on by a separate company. Profits and gains arising in respect of the business are generally exempt from corporation tax (although a tax charge may arise in certain tax avoidance cases or where a company fails to meet certain debt funding requirements or where it pays a dividend to a person with a 10% or more interest in the company). Profits of the company which are not from the tax-exempt business are chargeable to corporation tax at the main rate (currently 30%). To the extent that dividends paid by the company derive from ring-fenced profits and gains they are taxed in the hands of the recipient as property income rather than as distributions. Companies wishing to enter the regime must pay an entry charge. Companies may exit the regime at any time by notice, and may be required to do so by HMRC notice where they repeatedly fail to meet certain conditions. Exit from the regime is automatic where one or more of conditions (1), (2), (5) or (6) below cease to be met. The provisions apply in modified form to enable real estate investment trusts to participate in joint ventures and for groups of companies to become group real estate investment trusts. [FA 2006, ss 103–145, Schs 16, 17; ITA 2007, Sch 1 paras 616–621; FA 2007, s 52, Sch 17; SI 2006 Nos 2864–2867; SI 2007 Nos 3425, 3536, 3540]. For full coverage of the provisions see Tolley's Corporation Tax.'

65.7   **Qualified investor schemes.** The last paragraph on page 890 is amended to read as follows.

'Where the disposal would fall within one of the provisions listed below, the gain or loss calculated at the first measuring date is not deemed to accrue on the disposal. Instead, the transferee's holding in the QIS is treated as a substantial holding from the time of the disposal, and the gain or loss (or part thereof) is treated as accruing to the transferee on a disposal by him of all (or part) of the substantial holding. The provisions concerned are:

- *TCGA 1992, s 58(1)* (transfers between spouses or civil partners — see **42.4** MARRIED PERSONS AND CIVIL PARTNERS);

- *TCGA 1992, s 62(4)* (acquisition as legatee — see **18.9** DEATH);

- *TCGA 1992, s 139* (company reconstructions involving transfer of business — see **13.10** COMPANIES);

- *TCGA 1992, s 140A* (transfer or division of UK business between companies in different EC member states — see **45.10** OVERSEAS MATTERS);

- *TCGA 1992, s 140E* (European cross-border merger leaving assets within UK tax charge — see **45.11A** OVERSEAS MATTERS); and

- *TCGA 1992, s 171(1)* (intra-group transfers — see **27.2** GROUPS OF COMPANIES).'

66   Venture Capital Trusts

66.3   **The number of employees requirement.** The following paragraph is added at the end.

'HMRC consider that a full-time employee is one whose standard working week (excluding lunch breaks and overtime) is at least 35 hours (HMRC Venture Capital Schemes Manual VCM 15105).'

69   Tax Case Digest

The following cases are updated or added.

HMRC v Smallwood 15.6

Losses on disposal of units in enterprise zone unit trust — whether TCGA 1992, s 41(2) applicable.

In 1989 an individual (S) invested £10,000 in an enterprise zone unit trust. The trustees used the funds to acquire land and buildings, and claimed capital allowances. S was credited with some of these allowances under *Income Tax (Definition of Unit Trusts Schemes) Regulations 1988 (SI 1988 No 267)*. Subsequently, the property was disposed of and S received distributions, which were treated for CGT purposes as part disposals of S's units. S claimed that these disposals gave rise to allowable losses. The Revenue rejected the claim on the basis that the effect of *TCGA 1992, s 41(2)* was that S's allowable expenditure had to be restricted by the capital allowances. S appealed, contending that *section 41(2)* did not apply because it was the trustees' expenditure, rather than his expenditure, which gave rise to capital allowances. The Special Commissioner accepted this contention and allowed S's appeal, holding that 'once the step has been taken of treating the unit trust as a company and the rights of the unitholders as shares in that company, then for CGT purposes … the computation of gains on disposals of units must be treated in the same way as the computation of gains on disposals of shares'. Accordingly, the expression 'any expenditure to the extent to which any capital allowance … has been or may be made in respect of it' in *TCGA 1992, s 41(2)* had to be construed as 'referring to expenditure comprised in the consideration given wholly and exclusively for the acquisition of the relevant asset, i.e. the £10,000 given by (S) for his units. Capital allowances were not given in respect of that expenditure. Thus *section 41(2)* does not apply.' The CA unanimously upheld this decision. Lawrence Collins LJ held that the effect of *TCGA 1992, s 99* was 'that there are two levels of capital gains tax. First, gains made by the trustee in respect of trust assets are taxed as if they were gains of a company (except that the tax paid would not be corporation tax but capital gains tax). Any tax on these gains is assessed on the trustee. Second, each unit holder is treated on a disposal of his units as if they were shares in a company, his gains or losses on units being taxed as if they were gains or losses on shares.' *HMRC v Smallwood CA, [2007] STC 1237; [2007] EWCA Civ 462.*

Underwood v HMRC 15.2

'Bed and breakfast' transaction — whether disposal of land took place

In 1990 an individual (U) purchased some land for £1,400,000. In April 1993 he contracted to sell the land to a company (R) for £400,000. On the same day R gave him an option to repurchase the land for £400,000 plus 10% of any subsequent increase in its value. In November 1994 R contracted to sell the land to U for £420,000. On the same day U contracted to sell the property to a company (B) which he controlled. U appealed against CGT assessments for 1993/94 and 1994/95, contending that the April 1993 transactions had resulted in a CGT loss which could be set against gains he had made on the disposal of certain shares. The Special Commissioners and the Ch D rejected this contention and dismissed his appeal. Briggs J held that 'in reality all that happened was that the two contracts were settled by payment of a £20,000 difference, without any substantial performance of either of them'. Since there was 'no performance of either contract, there was therefore no transfer of the beneficial interest in the property under either contract, or at all'. *Underwood v HMRC, Ch D [2008] EWHC 108 (Ch), 2008 STI 219.*

Budget Summary 12 March 2008

Note: It must be remembered that these proposals are subject to amendment during the passage of the Finance Bill.

PERSONAL TAXATION	2008/09	2007/08
Personal allowance		
general	£5,435	£5,225
aged 65 or over in year		
of assessment	£9,030	£7,550
aged 75 or over in year		
of assessment	£9,180	£7,690
age allowance income limit	£21,800	£20,900
minimum where income		
exceeds limit	£5,435	£5,225
Married couple's allowance		
(10% relief)		
either partner born before		
6 April 1935	£6,535	£6,285
either partner aged 75 or		
over in year of assessment	£6,625	£6,365
age allowance income limit	£21,800	£20,900
minimum where income		
exceeds limit	£2,540	£2,440
Blind person's allowance	£1,800	£1,730
Income tax rates		
Starting rate	10%	10%
on income up to	£2,320*	£2,230
Basic rate	20%	22%
on taxable income		
up to	£36,000	£34,600
Higher rate	40%	40%
on taxable income over	£36,000	£34,600
Lower rate		
on certain savings income	–	20%
Lower rate on dividend income	10%	10%
Higher rate on dividend income	32.5%	32.5%

*Starting rate applies only to savings income for 2008/09. If taxable non-savings income is above this limit, the starting rate is not applicable.

COMPANY TAXATION	FY2008	FY2007
Corporation tax rates		
All companies (except below)	28%	30%
Companies with small profits	21%	20%
— 21%/20% rate limit	£300,000	£300,000
— marginal relief limit	£1,500,000	£1,500,000
— marginal relief fraction	7/400	1/40
— marginal rate	29.75%	32.5%

For certain profits from oil activities, the full rate and small profits rate are 30% and 19% respectively for both years, the marginal relief fraction is 11/400 and the marginal rate is 32.75%.

CAPITAL GAINS TAX	2008/09	2007/08
Rate — general	18%*	10%*:20%*:40%*
— trustees and personal		
representatives	18%*	40%*
General exemption limit	£9,600	£9,200
*subject to available reliefs		

INHERITANCE TAX	Transfers after 5/4/2008
Threshold	£312,000
(previously £300,000 for transfers after 5 April 2007)	
Death rate	40%

VAT

Standard rate	17.5%
Registration threshold after 31 March 2008	£67,000
(previously £64,000 after 31 March 2007)	

NATIONAL INSURANCE	2008/09

(2007/08 in brackets where different)

Class 1 contributions

Not contracted out
The employee contribution is 11% of earnings between £105 (£100) and £770 (£670) p.w. plus 1% of all earnings above £770 (£670) p.w. The employer contribution is 12.8% of all earnings in excess of the first £105 (£100) p.w.

Contracted out
The 'not contracted out' rates for employees are reduced on the band of earnings from £105 (£100) p.w. to £770 (£670) p.w. by 1.6%. For employers, they are reduced on the band of earnings from £105 (£100) p.w. to £770 (£670) p.w. by 3.7% for employees in salary-related schemes or 1.4% for employees in money purchase schemes. In addition, there is an employee rebate of 1.6% and an employer rebate of 3.7% or 1.4%, as appropriate, on earnings from £90 (£87) p.w. up to £105 (£100) p.w.

Class 1A and 1B contributions		12.8%

Class 2 contributions		
Flat weekly rate	£2.30	(£2.20)
Exemption limit	£4,825	(£4,635)

Class 3 contributions		
Flat weekly rate	£8.10	(£7.80)

Class 4 contributions
8% on the band of profits between £5,435 (£5,225) and £40,040 (£34,840) *plus* 1% on all profits above £40,040 (£34,840).

ADMINISTRATION OF TAX

Waiving Interest and Surcharges for Those Affected by National Disasters

HMRC are to be given power to allow interest and surcharges payable to them to be waived by secondary legislation in the context of events designated as national disasters.

The measure will have effect from the date that Finance Act 2008 receives Royal Assent but the power will first be used, with retrospective effect, to waive interest, etc. as a result of the severe flooding that affected the UK in June and July 2007.

Penalties for Incorrect Returns and Failure to Notify a Taxable Activity

Legislation will be introduced in Finance Bill 2008 to extend the current HMRC powers across all the taxes, levies and duties administered by HMRC in order to:

- create a single penalty regime for incorrect returns; and
- cover penalties for failing to register or notify HMRC of a new taxable activity.

The penalty regime for incorrect returns is expected to apply to return periods commencing after 31 March 2009 where the return is due to be filed after 31 March 2010. Penalties for failure to notify are expected to have effect for failure to meet notification obligations that arise after 31 March 2009.

For incorrect returns, there will be no penalty where a taxpayer makes a mistake but there will be a penalty of up to:

- 30% for failure to take reasonable care;
- 70% for a deliberate understatement; and
- 100% for a deliberate understatement with concealment.

Where a return is incorrect because a third party has deliberately provided false information or deliberately withheld information from the taxpayer, with the intention of causing an understatement of tax due, there will be a provision allowing a penalty to be charged on the third party.

For failure to notify a taxable activity there will be no penalty where there is no tax and/or NICs unpaid as a result or where the taxpayer has a reasonable excuse for the failure. Otherwise there will be a penalty of:

- 30% of tax unpaid for non-deliberate failure to notify;
- 70% of tax unpaid for a deliberate failure to notify; and
- 100% of tax unpaid for a deliberate failure with concealment.

All penalties will be substantially reduced where the taxpayer makes a disclosure, more so if this is unprompted.

For Class 2 NICs, the provisions will replace the fixed penalty of £100 for notification more than three months after starting self-employment with a behaviour-based penalty.

Compliance Checks

The rules for checking that businesses and individuals have paid the correct amount of IT, CGT, CT, VAT and PAYE or claimed the correct reliefs and allowances are to be reformed.

There will be three elements:

- the alignment and modernisation of record keeping requirements;
- new inspection and information powers; and
- the alignment and modernisation of time limits for making tax assessments and claims.

Information powers and penalties for failure to comply with these obligations will have effect after 31 March 2009. Time limits for making assessments and claims will need a transitional period and so will become fully operative after 31 March 2010.

Payments, Repayments and Debt

Measures will be introduced to make it easier for taxpayers to pay what they owe on time and for HMRC to tackle those who pay late or not at all. The three changes to the current law will:

- enable HMRC to introduce a credit card payment service (from Autumn 2008);

- allow HMRC to set the repayments it must make to individuals and businesses against the payments it is owed by them (from the date of Royal Assent to Finance Act 2008); and

- modernise and align HMRC's debt enforcement powers to collect unpaid sums by taking control of goods in England and Wales (in line with the appointed day for Tribunals, Courts and Enforcement Act 2007, Sch 12) or by taking action through the civil courts (from the date of Royal Assent to Finance Act 2008).

Indirect Taxes: Increase in Limit for Correction of Errors

The limits below which a business may adjust a current return to reflect errors on previous returns are to be increased. The revised limits take effect in relation to accounting periods commencing on or after 1 July 2008.

The revised limits, which apply to Value Added Tax (VAT), Insurance Premium Tax (IPT), Air Passenger Duty (APD), Landfill Tax (LFT), Climate Change Levy (CCL) and Aggregates Levy (AGL), are as follows:

- VAT, LFT, CCL and AGL: the greater of £10,000 and 1% of net VAT turnover (Box 6 of the VAT return) for the return period, subject to an upper limit of £50,000; LFT, CCL and AGL taxpayers who are not VAT registered will have a single limit of £10,000;

- IPT: the greater of £10,000 and 1% of net IPT turnover (Box 10 of the IPT return) subject to an upper limit of £50,000;

- APD: the greater of £10,000 and 1% of the duty due, before adjustments from previous periods, subject to an upper limit of £50,000.

The relevant regulations will be amended by statutory instrument.

PERSONAL TAXATION

Income Tax Rates and Allowances

For 2008/09, the basic rate of income tax is reduced from 22% to 20%. The 20% savings rate is merged with the basic rate. The 10% starting rate is abolished and a new 10% starting rate for savings is introduced. There is no change to the 40% higher rate of tax. The 10% dividend ordinary rate and the 32.5% dividend upper rate also remain unchanged.

The basic rate limit is increased to £36,000. The new 10% starting rate limit for savings is £2,320. However, this rate is not applicable if an individual's taxable non-savings income exceeds that limit; instead, the individual's savings income is taxed at the 20% basic rate up to the basic rate limit and at the 40% higher rate thereafter.

The basic personal allowance is increased to £5,435. Age-related personal allowances are £9,030 (for individuals aged 65 to 74) and £9,180 (for individuals aged 75 and over).

Income Shifting

Following the recent consultation on proposals to introduce legislation to prevent individuals shifting part of their income to another person who is subject to a lower rate of tax, the Government will not now enact legislation effective from 6 April 2008 but will conduct further consultation with the intention of including legislation in Finance Bill 2009.

Residence in the UK

For 2008/09 onwards, in deciding if an individual is resident in the UK for tax purposes, any day on which he is present in the UK at midnight will be counted as a day of presence in the UK for residence test purposes. Note that this is different from the earlier proposal that days of arrival and days of departure should each count as a day of presence. Days spent in transit will not count as days of presence, even if they involve being in the UK at midnight, so long as during transit the individual does not engage in activities inconsistent with his merely being in transit.

Residence and Domicile: Remittance Basis

The following changes are to be made to the remittance basis of taxation. The legislation will be in Finance Bill 2008 and will have effect for 2008/09 onwards.

- If he has been UK resident in more than seven out of the last ten tax years, an individual aged 18 or over who is non-domiciled or not ordinarily resident in the UK will be able to use the remittance basis for that tax year only if he pays an additional tax charge of £30,000 for that year. The charge will not, however, apply if the individual's unremitted foreign income and capital gains for the tax year is less than £2,000. Anyone who opts not to pay the additional charge will be taxed on their worldwide income and gains. The £30,000 charge will be collected through the self-assessment system and normal payment dates will apply. It will be regarded as a tax charge on the individual's unremitted income and gains. If the individual pays the £30,000 from an offshore source directly to HMRC it will not itself be treated as a taxable remittance.

- UK residents using the remittance basis for any tax year will not be entitled to UK personal reliefs or the capital gains annual exemption. This rule will operate independently of whether they are liable to, and have opted to pay, the £30,000 charge but will not apply to an individual whose unremitted foreign income and gains for the tax year is less than £2,000.

- Works of art will not be taxed under the remittance basis when brought into the UK for public display.

- An earlier legislative error is to be corrected. The error (in ITTOIA 2005) had the effect of charging income tax on foreign dividends at the rate of 32.5% for users of the remittance basis. The intention was always that foreign dividend income remitted to the UK should be taxed at 40%. The rate is duly increased to 40% for remittances made on or after 6 April 2008.

A number of loopholes in the remittance basis will be closed, for example:

- it will no longer be possible to remit income tax-free by claiming the remittance basis for the year the income arises but not for the year it is remitted;

- there will be measures to reduce the scope for converting taxable income and gains into non-taxable receipts through the use of offshore structures such as companies and trusts and the use of close relatives;

- certain pre-existing anti-avoidance legislation will be extended to apply to non-domiciled individuals;

- a pre-existing rule which does not permit income to be taxed in a year after the source has ceased will be abolished; and

- the definition of 'remittance' will be extended to cover in all cases items other than cash; certain assets owned on 11 March 2008 will be exempted.

Capital gains tax legislation will be amended so that non-domiciled individuals not being taxed on the remittance basis can obtain relief for foreign capital losses. Individuals who claim the remittance basis for any year from 2008/09 onwards will be able to obtain relief for such losses in any year for which they do not claim the remittance basis, but can do so only by making an irrevocable election that will require them to disclose details of unremitted gains.

Subject to grandfathering provisions for certain pre-existing mortgages, where a loan from a non-UK institution is advanced into the UK and is repaid out of untaxed foreign income, the repayments will count as remittances on and after 6 April 2008.

EMPLOYMENT TAXATION

Company Car Benefit

A new lower rate is to be introduced on the tax benefit of a company car made available for an employee's private use, from 6 April 2008. The taxable benefit is calculated on a percentage of the car's list price (the percentage being related to the CO2 emissions of the car).

The lower rate of 10% (13% for most diesels) will apply to cars with CO2 emissions of 120g/km or less.

The 15% lower threshold will be 135g/km for 2008/09 and 2009/10 and 130g/km from 2010/11.

Van Fuel Benefit

The rules for reimbursement of fuel purchased for business travel in company vans are to be aligned with those for company car fuel, with effect from Royal Assent to Finance Act 2008. The amount reimbursed will not be treated as earnings for tax purposes.

Residence and Domicile: Changes for Employment-related Securities

Legislation is to be introduced to ensure that the income tax charge in respect of employment-related securities operates in broadly the same way for employees who are UK resident but not ordinarily resident as it does for employees who are both resident and ordinarily resident in the UK. Where an employee is taxable on the remittance basis by virtue of his being not ordinarily resident, the amount otherwise chargeable in respect of employment-related securities will be apportioned, and any proportion relating to overseas duties will be charged on the remittance basis. A similar apportionment will be available to individuals not domiciled in the UK where the amount otherwise chargeable relates to a foreign employment the duties of which are performed wholly outside the UK. The legislation will have effect for 2008/09 onwards but not so as to affect securities acquired or options granted before 6 April 2008.

BUSINESS TAX

Capital Allowances: Plant and Machinery Allowance Regime; Special Rate Pool

As part of the business tax reform package announced at Budget 2007, the following changes will be introduced to the plant and machinery capital allowances regime from 1 April 2008 (corporation tax) or 6 April 2008 (income tax):

- the main rate of writing-down allowances (WDAs) will be reduced to 20% (previously 25%);

- the rate of WDAs on long-life assets will be increased to 10% (previously 6%);

- a new annual investment allowance (AIA) will be introduced for the first £50,000 of expenditure on most plant and machinery each year. Where more than £50,000 is spent in a chargeable period, the excess will qualify for WDAs in the normal manner. (This AIA is intended to complement any existing 100% first-year allowance (FYA) schemes. Any expenditure that qualifies for 100% allowances under separate schemes will be unaffected by the introduction of the AIA); and

- where unrelieved expenditure in the main pool is £1,000 or less, businesses can claim a WDA of any amount up to £1,000.

In addition, a new 10% 'special rate' pool will be introduced into which capital expenditure on the following assets will be allocated:

- any unrelieved expenditure in a pre-FA 2008 long-life asset pool;

- expenditure on the thermal insulation of a building (previously such expenditure qualified for 25% allowances, but only when incurred on an industrial building); and

- expenditure on certain 'integral features'. (Currently listed as electrical systems (including lighting systems); cold water systems; space or water heating systems, powered systems of ventilation, air cooling or air purification and any floor or ceiling comprised in such systems; lifts, escalators and moving walkways; external solar shading; and active facades).

As for the main pool, where the unrelieved expenditure in the 'special rate' pool is £1,000 or less, businesses can claim a WDA of any amount up to £1,000.

Capital Allowances: Enterprise Zone Allowances, Industrial Buildings Allowances and Agricultural Buildings Allowances

As previously announced, enterprise zone allowances (EZAs) are to be withdrawn from April 2011. The EZA withdrawal is similar to the withdrawal of the agricultural buildings allowances (ABAs) and industrial buildings allowances (IBAs) introduced in FA 2007, except that:

- EZAs will not be subject to the phasing out rules which will apply to the IBAs and ABAs; and

- balancing charges in respect of EZAs will be retained for a limited period, such that where a business disposes of a building within 7 years of first use (and allowances have been claimed), then the business will still potentially be liable to a balancing charge.

FA 2008 will also contain detailed rules on:

- the phasing out of WDAs for expenditure on industrial and agricultural buildings (broadly the amount of WDA is to be stepped down by 25% for each financial or tax year, from 1 April 2008); and

- specific anti-avoidance provisions counteracting disclosed schemes aimed at exploiting the legislation withdrawing balancing adjustments in order to claim multiple WDAs.

Draft legislation has been published and is available on the HMRC website.

First-year Allowances for Natural Gas, Biogas and Hydrogen Refuelling Equipment

The 100% first-year allowance available for expenditure incurred on natural gas and hydrogen refuelling equipment for vehicles will be extended until 31 March 2013 (previously due to end on 31 March 2008). From 1 April 2008, the allowance will also apply to refuelling equipment for biogas.

First-year Allowances for Expenditure on Low-emission Cars

The 100% first-year allowance for qualifying expenditure on new cars with CO2 emissions not exceeding 120g/km will be extended until 31 March 2013. In addition, the definition of a qualifying low-CO2 car will be amended. For expenditure incurred on or after 1 April 2008, the qualifying emissions threshold will be reduced to 110g/km. Low-emissions cars costing more than £12,000 are not treated as falling in a single-asset pool. A transitional rule will apply in relation to leases entered into before 1 April 2008, to ensure that cars with emissions below the current threshold but above the new threshold are unaffected by the reduction.

Capital Allowances: First-year Tax Credits

New measures will enable loss-making companies to surrender losses in exchange for a cash payment (a first-year tax credit) from the Government, provided:

- the losses are attributable to 100% first-year allowances on designated energy-saving or environmentally beneficial plant and machinery;
- the loss cannot be otherwise relieved by the company; and
- the qualifying expenditure was incurred on or after 1 April 2008.

The credit that will be paid to the company will be 19% of the loss surrendered, although it cannot exceed the greater of:

- the total of the company's PAYE and NIC for the loss period; or
- £250,000.

Any first-year tax credits will be clawed back if the qualifying plant and machinery is sold within 4 years of the end of the period in which the tax credit was paid.

Capital Allowances Buying and Acceleration

New measures will counter the avoidance of corporation tax through the use of arrangements designed to crystallise a balancing allowance on plant and machinery involving the sale of a trade to a profitable group which does not intend to carry on the trade in the long term. An example of this is where a loss-making company is sold to an unconnected profitable group prior to the trade (rather than the company) being sold to a third party some time later. The new measures will ensure that the sale of the trade does not lead to a balancing allowance in the hands of the profitable company. The rules will take effect where a company sells its trade on or after 12 March 2008.

Trading Stock

Finance Bill 2008 will provide that, where goods are appropriated into or from trading stock other than by way of trade, the profits of the trade should be adjusted for tax purposes to replace the cost of the stock, or the actual proceeds, with their market value. This is intended to give statutory effect to a long-established, non-statutory rule.

Leased Plant or Machinery: Anti-avoidance

Legislation is to be introduced to counter avoidance by businesses acting as intermediate lessors, leasing in plant or machinery under one lease and leasing it out under another. The avoidance exploits differences in the way the two leases are taxed, which allow the business, as lessee, to deduct all the lease rentals payable but tax the business, as lessor, on only a portion of rentals receivable, thus creating an artificial loss. The legislation will ensure that rentals received are taxed on the same basis as rentals paid.

Legislation will also be introduced to counter avoidance involving leases of plant or machinery granted in return for a capital payment, often described as a premium, which escapes taxation because it does not have to be brought in as a disposal receipt for capital allowances purposes and because little or no tax would be payable under the chargeable gains regime. The legislation will ensure that such payments are normally to be taxed as income of the lessor. It will also counter attempts to reduce or avoid a capital allowances disposal receipt on the granting of a long funding finance lease where these rely on reducing the value of the leased asset as shown in the lessor's balance sheet.

In addition, in the case of a sale and finance leaseback, the finance lease will in most cases be treated as a long funding lease, with ensuing tax consequences. Lease and finance leasebacks will be treated in similar fashion.

In all cases the legislation will generally have effect for transactions entered into after 12 December 2007 but certain aspects of it have effect only after 11 March 2008.

Restrictions on Trade Loss Relief for Individuals

Legislation is already in place to counter the use of partnership arrangements that generate trade losses for use as 'sideways loss relief' by a non-active or limited partner. 'Sideways loss relief' means the set-off of trading losses against income other than from the trade and against chargeable gains. Similar action is now to be taken against individuals who are not in partnership but carry on a trade in a 'non-active capacity'. Where a loss arises to such an individual as a result of tax avoidance arrangements made on or after 12 March 2008, no sideways loss relief will be available. Where this is not the case, there will nevertheless be an annual limit of £25,000 on the total sideways loss relief that an individual can claim from trades carried on in a non-active capacity. Transitional rules will apply where the individual's basis period straddles 12 March 2008. The restrictions will not apply to losses derived from certain film reliefs or to Lloyd's underwriting losses. For these purposes an individual carries on a trade in a non-active capacity if he spends an average of less than 10 hours a week personally engaged in commercial activities of the trade. Legislation will also align the existing definition of 'non-active partner' with this new definition.

CORPORATION TAX

Corporation Tax Main Rates

The main rate of corporation tax, chargeable when a company's profits exceed £1.5m, will be 28% with effect from 1 April 2009. The main rate applicable to profits of companies from certain oil and gas ring fence activities will remain unchanged at 30% from 1 April 2009.

Corporation Tax Small Companies' Rates

The small companies' rate of corporation tax will be increased from 20% to 21% with effect from 1 April 2008. The fraction used in calculating marginal small companies' relief will become 7/400 but there will be no change to the lower and upper profit limits of £300,000 and £1.5m.

The small companies' rate applicable to ring-fence profits from certain oil and gas activities will remain at 19% from 1 April 2008, and there will be no change to the marginal small companies' relief fraction of 11/400 for such profits.

Associated Companies Rules

Changes will be made to the associated companies rules as they apply to the small companies' rate (SCR) of corporation tax. The changes will amend the definition of 'control', solely for the purposes of SCR, to ensure that the rights or powers held by business partners will be attributed only when there have been tax planning arrangements involving the shareholder or director and the partner to secure a tax advantage by virtue of greater relief under the SCR rules. These changes will apply with effect from 1 April 2008.

Research and Development and Vaccine Research Relief Schemes

The following amendments are to be made to the Research and Development (R&D) scheme and the Vaccine Research Relief (VRR) scheme.

Research and Development relief scheme:

- from a date to be announced the rates of R&D relief are to be increased to 175% for SME's and 130% for large companies (previously 150% and 125% respectively);

- the amount of relief available under the SME scheme is to be restricted to Euro 7.5m per R&D project.

Vaccine Research Relief (VRR) scheme:

- the amount of relief available under the VRR scheme will be reduced to 40% (currently 50%);

- the amount of relief available under the VRR scheme is to be restricted to Euro 7.5m per R&D project;

- large companies will have to make a declaration concerning the incentive effect of any relief they are claiming under the VRR scheme.

In addition, legislation will be introduced to prevent companies from claiming R&D and/or VRR relief if their most recent accounts are not prepared on a going concern basis.

Controlled Foreign Companies: Anti-avoidance

Finance Bill 2008 will include provisions to block a number of artificial avoidance schemes that rely on the use of a partnership or a trust to escape a controlled foreign company (CFC) charge either by misusing one of the exemptions from the CFC rules or by arranging for profits to be earned in such a way that they purportedly fall outside the scope of the rules.

The changes will have effect on or after 12 March 2008. For changes that are relevant to an accounting period, the measures will provide that, for accounting periods that straddle that date, the accounting period will be split into periods before and from that date with the changes only having effect to the second part of that accounting period.

Corporate Intangible Assets Regime: Anti-avoidance

Finance Bill 2008 will include provisions to clarify that the effect of the 'related party' rules in the corporate intangible assets regime in FA 2002, Sch 29 is unaffected by any administration, liquidation or other insolvency proceedings or equivalent arrangements that any company or partnership may be involved in. The measure will have effect for transactions made in respect of intangible assets (including royalties becoming payable) on or after 12 March 2008.

CAPITAL GAINS

Capital Gains Tax Reform

As previously announced, major changes to capital gains tax are to be included in Finance Bill 2008. The proposed changes are to apply to disposals on or after 6 April 2008 and will not apply for the purposes of corporation tax on chargeable gains. The main changes are as follows.

- A single tax rate of 18% will apply to individuals, trustees and personal representatives.
- Taper relief will be withdrawn both for disposals on or after 6 April 2008 and deferred gains coming into charge on or after that date.
- Indexation allowance will be withdrawn.
- All assets held on 31 March 1982 will be deemed to have been acquired on that date at market value (i.e. rebasing will apply automatically to all assets).
- Simplified identification rules for shares and securities will apply.

Relief on Disposal of a Business

A new capital gains tax relief ('entrepreneurs' relief') will be introduced for disposals on or after 6 April 2008. The relief will apply to the disposal by an individual of:

- all or part of a trade carried on alone or in partnership;
- assets of such a trade following cessation; or
- shares or securities in the individual's personal trading company (as defined).

Where a disposal of shares or of an interest in the assets of a partnership qualifies for relief, an associated disposal of assets owned by the individual and used by the company or partnership also qualifies for relief.

Trustees will be able to claim relief on certain disposals of business assets or shares where a qualifying beneficiary has an interest in the business concerned.

Budget Summary

The relief will be available where the relevant conditions are met throughout a period of one year and will operate by reducing the amount of qualifying gains by four-ninths (so that the gains are effectively charged to CGT at 10%). Relief will be subject to a lifetime limit of gains of £1 million, but disposals before 6 April 2008 will not count towards the limit. Relief given to trustees will count towards the limit of the qualifying beneficiary.

Transitional rules will apply to allow relief to be claimed in certain circumstances where a gain made before 6 April 2008 is deferred and becomes chargeable on or after that date.

Consequential Changes following Transferability of IHT Nil-rate Band

As announced in the Pre-Budget Report, legislation will be introduced in Finance Bill 2008 to allow any IHT nil-rate band unused on a person's death to be transferred to the estate of their spouse or civil partner who dies after 8 October 2007.

With effect from 6 April 2008, an amendment will be made to TCGA 1992, s 274 (which provides that where the value of an asset in a deceased person's estate has been ascertained for IHT purposes, that value also has effect for CGT purposes) to ensure that it will not have effect where the valuation of an asset does not have to be ascertained for IHT purposes on the death of an individual. So, for example, if the IHT valuation of an asset does not have to be ascertained until the death of the surviving spouse in order to establish the nil-rate band that may be transferred, TCGA 1992, s 274 will not require that value to be used for any CGT calculation.

SAVINGS AND INVESTMENTS

Venture Capital Schemes

The maximum amount on which an investor can obtain relief under the Enterprise Investment Scheme (EIS) in any tax year is to be increased from £400,000 to £500,000. This is, however, subject to State aid approval by the European Commission, so both the increase itself and the start date are not yet certain.

For the purposes of the EIS, the Venture Capital Trust (VCT) scheme and the Corporate Venturing Scheme (CVS), the activities of shipbuilding and coal and steel production are to become excluded activities. As a result, investors will not be able to obtain tax relief under these three schemes for investments in companies carrying on any of these activities. For the EIS and CVS this will apply to shares issued on or after 6 April 2008. For VCTs it applies in relation to money raised on or after that date (but not money derived from the investment of money raised before that date).

Enterprise Management Incentives

At present employees cannot hold qualifying Enterprise Management Incentive (EMI) options with a total market value of more than £100,000 at date of grant (taking into account any Company Share Option Plan options also granted to them). For options granted on or after 6 April 2008, this limit is to be increased to £120,000.

For options granted on or after the date of Royal Assent to Finance Act 2008, EMIs will be limited to qualifying companies with fewer than 250 full-time employees. (If a company has part-time employees, a reasonable fraction for each one counts toward the 250 limit.)

Companies involved in shipbuilding, coal and steel production are to be precluded from offering EMIs, though this will not affect options granted before the date of Royal Assent to Finance Act 2008.

Investment Manager Exemption

Finance Bill 2008 will introduce changes to the legislation underpinning the Investment Manager Exemption (IME), which enables non-residents to appoint UK-based investment managers to carry out transactions on their behalf without the risk of exposure to UK tax, provided that certain conditions are met. HMRC will be allowed to make an order designating transactions as 'investment transactions' for the purposes of the IME. There will then be a single list of such transactions, which will be available on the HMRC website. In addition, where not all of the transactions carried out in the UK by an investment manager on behalf of a non-resident meet the qualifying conditions, only the non-qualifying transactions will be exposed to UK tax.

Personal Dividends from Non-UK Resident Companies

At present, individuals receiving dividends from non-UK resident companies are not entitled to a tax credit as they would be if the dividend came from a UK resident company. For 2008/09 UK resident individuals and UK and other EEA nationals will be entitled to such tax credits if they own less than a 10% shareholding in the distributing non-UK resident company. The tax credit will be one-ninth of the distribution and will be non-repayable. It was previously announced that such individuals would be entitled to the tax credit only if their total dividends from non-resident companies was less than £5,000 but this condition has now been dropped.

For 2009/10 onwards, the 10% shareholding condition will no longer apply but tax credits on dividends from non-UK resident companies will be available only if the source country levies a tax on corporate profits similar to UK corporation tax. There will be anti-avoidance measures to deter abuse.

Offshore Funds: New Tax Regime

Legislation will be introduced in Finance Bill 2008 providing for regulations dealing with the taxation of investors in offshore funds.

Currently, offshore funds are required to distribute at least 85% of their income to be regarded as 'qualifying funds'. Such funds offer investors disposing of their interest favourable tax treatment (the disposal is liable to capital gains tax or corporation tax on chargeable gains, rather than income tax/corporation tax on income, as would otherwise be the case). With effect from a date to be appointed, offshore funds will no longer have to make a distribution but will instead be able to 'report' income to investors, who will be subject to tax on that income.

Draft regulations, to be published shortly after the Finance Bill, will set out the conditions which an offshore fund must meet to ensure that the disposal of an interest obtains favourable tax treatment.

Property Authorised Investment Funds

New regulations will be introduced to provide a tax regime for investment into real property and certain property companies, which will enable certain authorised investment funds to elect for a tax treatment that will move the point of taxation from the fund to its investors. The regulations will enable a Property Authorised Investment Fund to provide an open-ended fund alternative to the existing closed-ended UK Real Estate Investment Trusts. Funds will have to meet certain conditions in order to qualify for the new regime. They will have to be incorporated as an open-ended investment company, and carry on a property investment business which amounts to at least 60% of the business. They must meet a 'genuine diversity of ownership' condition, so that the fund is not limited to or targeted at only a few specified investors. There will also be limits on the holdings of corporate investors and on the type and amount of loan financing in the fund.

Overseas Pension Schemes

Internationally mobile workers in the UK and their employers can obtain tax relief on contributions to non-registered pension schemes based outside the UK. Measures will be introduced to ensure that funds in non-UK schemes that have received UK tax relief are correctly identified for the purposes of the UK tax rules, so that the amount of an employer's contribution will not affect the calculation of the proportion of an individual's pension fund that is subject to UK tax rules. For overseas money-purchase schemes this will have effect for employer contributions paid after 11 March 2008, and for overseas defined-benefit schemes from 6 April 2008.

Pensions and Inheritance Tax

An IHT charge will arise on an unauthorised lump sum payment in respect of a pension scheme member in receipt of an annuity or scheme pension, who dies aged 75 or older, on or after 6 April 2008. Any balance of IHT nil-rate band not already used against their estate may be set against the charge. This treatment will also apply to alternatively secured pensions.

Legislation will also be introduced in Finance Bill 2008 to restore IHT protection to UK tax-relieved pension savings in overseas pensions schemes and all savings in certain overseas pension schemes, backdated to 6 April 2006.

Northern Rock ISAs

Finance Bill 2008 will include legislation to allow individuals who withdrew cash from their Northern Rock ISAs between 13 and 19 September 2007 to reinvest them in a new ISA between 18 October 2007 and 5 April 2008.

Manufactured Payments

Finance Bill 2008 will include a targeted anti-avoidance rule, with retrospective effect from 31 January 2008, to deny relief for any manufactured payment paid as part of a scheme or arrangements where one of the main purposes is to secure a tax advantage.

INHERITANCE TAX

Inheritance Tax: Transitional Serial Interests

FA 2006, Sch 20 changed the IHT rules for interest in possession (IIP) trusts. But it included a transitional period (from 22 March 2006 to 5 April 2008) to enable trustees to reorganise trusts set up before 22 March 2006 without being subject to the new rules. As the effect of the transitional provisions is unclear where pre-22 March 2006 IIP trusts are replaced with a 'transitional serial interest' (as defined) for the same beneficiary, legislation will be introduced in Finance Bill 2008 to clarify the position. It will ensure that the new rules will not have effect where this kind of change is made in the transitional period but will also ensure that the new rules will have effect as intended where an IIP trust is replaced after the transitional period with a new IIP trust (for either the same or a different beneficiary).

In addition, the transitional period will be extended by 6 months to 5 October 2008.

CHARITIES

Gift Aid

The reduction in the basic rate of income tax from 22% to 20% for 2008/09 onwards has the consequential effect of reducing the amount of tax a charity can claim back from HMRC in respect of Gift Aid donations received. For three years only, i.e. 2008/09, 2009/10 and 2010/11, a charity can claim back the difference. For a donation of £78, for example, a charity could previously claim back £22 (£78 x 22/78). It will now be able to claim back only £19.50 under normal rules (£78 x 20/80) but can claim back the extra £2.50 under these transitional rules. The claim must be made within set time limits.

TRUSTS

Income of Beneficiaries under Settlor-interested Trusts

The income of a trust in which the settlor has an interest is treated for income tax purposes as the settlor's income. Tax paid by the trustees is treated as paid on his behalf. Measures are already in place to avoid the double taxation that would otherwise arise when the income is distributed to beneficiaries. As a further measure, with backdated effect for 2006/07 onwards, the distribution will be treated as one of the highest slices of the beneficiary's income so that it will not have the unintended effect of pushing his savings and/or dividend income into a higher rate band.

STAMP TAXES

Stamp Duty: Changes to Loan Capital Exemption

Finance Bill 2008 will provide exemption from stamp duty on transfers of loan capital which are subject to a capital market arrangement on limited recourse terms. This will have effect from the date of Royal Assent.

Reduction of Stamp Duty Administrative Burden

With effect from 13 March 2008, instruments transferring stocks and shares that were previously chargeable with £5 stamp duty will be exempt, and will not need to be presented to HMRC for stamping.

Alternative Finance

Finance Bill 2008 will include legislation to classify certain alternative finance investment bonds which are similar to debt securities ('sukuk') as loan capital for stamp duty purposes. This will take effect from the date of Royal Assent.

SDLT: Relief for New Zero-carbon Flats

From 1 October 2007 to 30 September 2012, new zero-carbon flats will qualify for relief from SDLT. The relief will remove all SDLT liabilities for new zero-carbon flats up to a purchase price of £500,000. Where the purchase price exceeds £500,000, the SDLT liability will be reduced by £15,000 and the balance of the SDLT liability will be due in the normal way. The relief will only apply to the first sale of new flats. It will not apply to second and subsequent sales, or to existing flats even where they are converted to meet the zero-carbon criteria.

Where a Government department carries out an assessment of whether a home meets the zero-carbon standard, it will be permitted to charge a reasonable fee for this service.

SDLT: Thresholds

From 12 March 2008, the threshold for when a person has to notify HMRC of a non-leasehold land transaction will be raised from £1,000 to £40,000. Transactions involving leases for 7 years or more will only have to be notified where any chargeable consideration other than rent is more than £40,000, or where the annual rent is more than £1,000.

The provisions of FA 2003 which are intended to prevent the manipulation of lease thresholds will also be amended. For non-residential properties where the annual rent on a lease is £1,000 or more and a premium is paid, the normal 0% threshold that would have effect at £150,000 is withdrawn, and SDLT is charged at 1%. For residential properties, the normal thresholds will apply to any premium paid regardless of what rent is paid, and the existing '£600 rule' will no longer have effect.

Agents will be allowed to sign certificates on form SDLT 60 that no SDLT is due.

SDLT: Partnerships

Finance Bill 2008 will include legislation, with retrospective effect from 19 July 2007, to amend the SDLT provisions concerning transfers of property between partners within investment partnerships. The changes are intended to ensure that there will be no charge to SDLT where there is a transfer of an interest in a property within an investment partnership.

SDLT: Group Relief

FA 2003, Sch 7, para 1, which allows companies to claim group relief on transfers of assets between group members, will be amended from 13 March 2008 to counter avoidance schemes which have been structured to avoid the 'clawback' provisions in the legislation. Where the vendor leaves the group and, within 3 years of the asset having been transferred, there is a subsequent change in the control of the purchaser, HMRC will be able to link these two events and treat the purchaser as having left the group first. Group relief will not be clawed back where only the vendor leaves the group.

SDLT: Financial Avoidance

Finance Bill 2008 will introduce legislation intended to counter avoidance schemes, designed to take advantage of relief under FA 2003, s 71A or 72, whereby financial institutions have colluded with vendors so that the ownership of a property has been placed in a subsidiary company of the financial institution. The legislation is intended to ensure that relief will not be available if there are arrangements in place for a person to acquire control of the financial institution involved in the transaction. It came into effect on 12 March 2008.

Disclosure of SDLT Avoidance Schemes

The SDLT avoidance scheme disclosure rules are to be extended by legislation later in 2008 to residential properties worth £1 million or more.

VALUE ADDED TAX

Registration and Deregistration

With effect from 1 April 2008, the VAT registration threshold will be increased from £64,000 to £67,000. The deregistration threshold will be increased from £62,000 to £65,000. The registration and deregistration thresholds for acquisitions from other EU member states will also be increased from £64,000 to £67,000.

Extension to the Exemption for Fund Management

With effect from 1 October 2008, the VAT exemption for fund management under VATA 1994, Sch 9, Group 5, items 9 and 10 will be extended to cover:

- closed-ended investment entities which invest in securites and whose shares are included in the UK Listing Authority main Official List;

- funds established outside the UK which are recognised overseas schemes under the Financial Services and Markets Act 2000, ss 264, 270 and 272.

Trust-based schemes will be deleted.

The measure will be introduced by secondary legislation. Draft legislation and guidance will appear on the HMRC website in April.

Car Fuel Scale Charges

The scale used to charge VAT on fuel used for private motoring in business cars will be amended from the start of the first VAT period beginning on or after 1 May 2008. The minimum and maximum CO_2 level bands are reduced to 120 g/km and 235 g/km respectively.

The revised charges are:

CO2 band g/km	VAT fuel scale charge		
	12-month period £	3-month period £	1-month period £
120 or below	555	138	46
135	830	207	69
140	885	221	73

CO2 band g/km	12-month period £	VAT fuel scale charge 3-month period £	1-month period £
145	940	234	78
150	995	248	82
155	1,050	262	87
160	1,105	276	92
165	1,160	290	96
170	1,215	303	101
175	1,270	317	105
180	1,325	331	110
185	1,380	345	115
190	1,435	359	119
195	1,490	373	124
200	1,545	386	128
205	1,605	400	133
210	1,660	414	138
215	1,715	428	142
220	1,770	442	147
225	1,825	455	151
230	1,880	469	156
235 or above	1,935	483	161

Emission figures which are not multiples of 5 are rounded down. In the case of bi-fuel cars which have two emission figures, the lower emission figure should be used. For cars with no emission figures, HMRC have prescribed a level of emissions by reference to the engine capacity.

Reduced Rate: Smoking Cessation Products

A reduced rate of 5% for 'over the counter' sales of smoking cessation products was introduced with effect from 1 July 2007, and was originally to apply for one year. Secondary legislation to be laid before Parliament will extend this relief for an unspecified period.

Transitional Period for Claims

Legislation is to be introduced in Finance Bill 2008 providing for a transitional period, ending on 31 March 2009, during which businesses may submit claims for:

- output tax overpaid before 4 December 1996; and
- input tax incurred prior to 1 May 1997 and not claimed.

This measure follows the House of Lords judgements in *Fleming* and *Condé Nast* to the effect that the three-year cap on input tax claims (introduced with effect from 1 May 1997) was ineffective since no transitional period had been provided. The Commissioners consider that the judgement applies equally to the three-year cap on claims for overpaid output tax, introduced with effect from 4 December 1996.

Corresponding measures will allow the Commissioners to raise an assessment where the payment of a claim is subsequently found to be incorrect. Such an assessment must be made within 2 years of the end of the accounting period in which the claim is made.

Option to Tax Land and Buildings

A revised Schedule 10 is to be inserted into VATA 1994. The change will be made by Treasury Order and will take effect on 1 June 2008.

The revised schedule will set out the circumstances in which an election to waive exemption (option to tax) may be revoked after 20 years. Since the option was introduced with effect from 1 August 1989, the earliest date for a revocation is 1 August 2009.

Budget Summary

To improve the administration of the option and its revocation, several other measures will be incorporated. These relate to:

- opted properties held in a VAT group;

- opted buildings acquired for use as dwellings or relevant residential purpose and bare land acquired for construction of building for such purposes;

- the introduction of a new option to simplify the option to tax process for taxpayers with a number of properties;

- early revocation of an option to tax within a 'cooling-off' period;

- the automatic lapse of an option to tax 6 years after the taxpayer ceased to have any interest in a property that they had previously opted to tax;

- the ability, in certain circumstances, to exclude a new building from a previous option to tax; and

- late applications for permission to opt to tax.

Supplies of Temporary Staff

The current VAT concession in respect of supplies of temporary staff by employment businesses is to be withdrawn with effect from 1 April 2009. From that date, VAT will be applied to the total consideration employment businesses receive, including the wages element, in respect of the supplies they make.